RAILWAY GUNS

RAILWAY GUNS

British and German Guns at War
John Goodwin

PEN & SWORD
TRANSPORT

First published in Great Britain in 2017 by
PEN & SWORD TRANSPORT
an imprint of
Pen & Sword Books Ltd,
47 Church Street,
Barnsley,
South Yorkshire,
S70 2AS

A CIP record for this book is available from the British Library.

ISBN 978 1 47385 411 6

Printed and bound in England by CPI Group (UK) Ltd, Croydon, CR0 4YY.

Pen & Sword Books Ltd incorporates the Imprints of Pen & Sword Aviation, Pen & Sword Maritime, Pen & Sword Military, Wharncliffe Local History, Pen & Sword Select, Pen & Sword Military Classics and Leo Cooper.

For a complete list of Pen & Sword titles please contact
Pen & Sword Books Limited
47 Church Street, Barnsley, South Yorkshire, S70 2AS, England

E-mail: enquiries@pen-and-sword.co.uk
Website: www.pen-and-sword.co.uk

Contents

Dedication

Written as a tribute to happy memories of my railway family in wartime. Joseph Frank Goodwin and my Mother, Amy Elizabeth.

Royal Engineers 1914–1918
Railway Home Guard 1940–1945
Southern Railway Company 1911–1959

And my brother, Harold Harcourt Goodwin
Royal Engineers WWII
British Railways Board, Southern Region 1946–1984

Also by John Goodwin who served in the Royal Signals 1943-1947:
Eastbourne Redoubt, 1976
S623.1

The Military Defence of West Sussex
ISBN 0 906520 23 1
Middleton Press, 1985

Fortifications of the South Coast
The Pevensey, Eastbourne and Newhaven Defences
ISBN 0 9524158 0 1
1994

Military Signals from the South Coast
ISBN 1 901706 54 0
Middleton Press, 2000

Defending Sussex Beaches 1940–1942
ISBN 978 1 906008 79 6
Middleton Press, 2010

Acknowledgements

The assembly of information about events, which took place seventy-five years ago, meant consulting many sources. There was inevitably repetition and it is sometimes difficult to trace where original information came from. I have drawn extensively on nineteenth- and twentieth-century printed matter, and the book list at the end represents the accounts I found most authentic and helpful. Many of the military illustrations have been in the public domain for a long time; many railway photographs were acquired with little or no indication of their origin. I am especially grateful to fellow members of the Fortress Study Group, The National Archives, the Royal Artillery Library, the Imperial War Museum, the Royal Engineers Institution, the Tank Museum, the National Railway Museum, and Dover Public Library History Centre. I gratefully acknowledge all those who helped me in this research, directly or indirectly, and give my thanks.

I was privileged to know the late Ian Hogg, Master Gunner of the Royal Artillery, and fellow member of the Fortress Study Group. He wrote many books about the history and performance of guns with the authority given by experience in combat.

Jonathan Wright, John Scott Morgan and Jodie Butterwood of Pen and Sword Books have been very helpful with advice and illustrations, support which is much appreciated.

Chapter 1

The First Working
Railway Gun in Britain

In the last half of the nineteenth century there was much public discussion in Victorian military journals about planning a railway network so that in time of war it could be used offensively to protect cities and the coast. One proposal was for a circular railway line around London for troops and artillery to be moved quickly to areas under attack. Other suggestions were to build or re-route lines close to the coast, from which railway guns could fire at ships or troops landing on the beaches. At this time all European nations were spending millions on fortifying their borders. One of the arguments advanced in Britain was that mounting guns on railway trucks would be less costly and more flexible than building extensive coastal fortifications, which might turn out to be in the wrong place.

On 8 April 1847 an inventor, Sir James Caleb Anderson from Cork, had applied to HM Chancery in Edinburgh for several patents, one of which was for long 32-pounder guns to be mounted on iron ordnance trucks which ran on rails. Two years later he prepared plans and estimates for guns so mounted to travel on railway lines close to the coast in Southern England. The Duke of Wellington who was Commander-in-Chief of the army saw these and was lukewarm about the idea which was to have cost more than £1 million. The experienced General Burgoyne who had responsibility for all the fortifications in the country dismissed this and similar proposals as impractical. In his view a few determined men with dynamite could easily put a railway line out of action. There was also no enthusiasm and downright obstruction from the Admiralty and War Office who were already committed to an expensive programme of fortifying the naval ports.

It was not until 1894, with private funding and cooperation between senior officers of the 1st Sussex Artillery Volunteers and the London, Brighton, and South Coast Railway, that the first working railway mounted gun carriage was designed and built at Brighton. It was to be used to give mobile artillery support to those defending the coast in the event of an attack. An Armstrong rifled breech-loading field gun was available from the near derelict fort at the mouth of Shoreham harbour. Adaptations were made to a 20-ton railway flat wagon at the Brighton railway works and the field gun with its carriage wheels intact was mounted on a turntable. To protect the crew they were enclosed in a steel tank-like structure with sides 1.8m high and 12mm thick. This clumsy contraption was anchored to the ground by cross girders and grapnels when the gun was fired but the turntable enabled it to be pointed in all directions.

Two locomotives to push the gun truck along and coaches for ammunition, stores and accommodation were also built in the 1890s at the Brighton works. The engines were designed by Robert J. Billinton and were Class D3 0-4-4 tank locomotives numbered 363 and 375. The gun truck had to be at the front of the train which caused some objections to be raised as strict Board of Trade regulations of the time stipulated that rolling stock had to be pulled and not pushed from the rear.

During the next few years the gun train took part in military exercises with the Sussex Artillery Volunteers at Newhaven, Arundel, and Sheffield Park in Sussex, and on the Elham Valley line in Kent. Near Newhaven harbour twelve rounds were fired a mile offshore into Seaford Bay.

Influential members of the establishment including generals and admirals were present at the demonstration, but the War Office never took up the idea and little was heard of it after 1900. At this time the Royal Navy was the most powerful in the world. Since 1860 priority and resources had been given to sustaining its superiority and making its harbours impregnable. It was not conceivable that an enemy could pose a serious threat to the British coast, which could not be defeated.

A late nineteenth-century field gun, manned by artillery volunteers.
(Author's Collection)

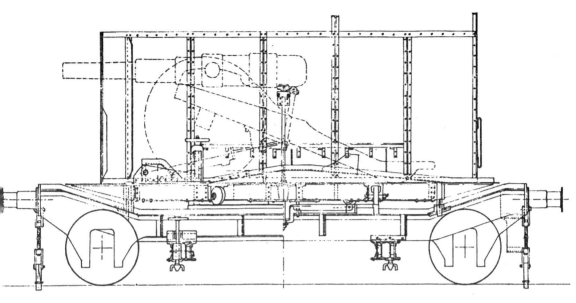

The 40-pounder Armstrong field gun mounted on a 20-ton railway flat truck, 7 metres long with its wheels slotted into sloping incline channels to absorb the recoil.

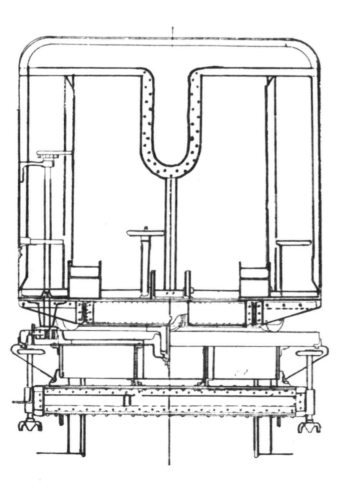

The front of the gun truck with a gun aperture and wheels allowing the turntable to traverse 360 degrees.

One of two engines that pushed the gun. An LB&SCR 0-4-4T tank locomotive
number 363, built at the Brighton Locomotive works to a design by R.J. Billinton.
(Author's Collection)

*An early photograph of
1st Sussex Artillery
Volunteers with their
railway gun.*

*Lord Charles Beresford
fires the Sussex railway
gun in 1894.*
(Author's Collection)

An armoured truck held ammunition and was defensible by riflemen.

General Burgoyne's view was that it was easy to put a railway out of action.

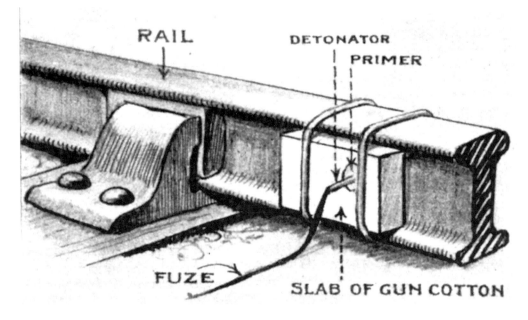

Chapter 2

The Short Active Life of British Railway Guns 1916–1918

A gun fires in a flat trajectory below 45°
A howitzer fires at angles above 45°

It was not until two years into the First World War that heavy railway mounted artillery was delivered to the British Army on the Western Front in France. Until then horse teams, tractors and half tracks pulled most guns into position, but as these got bigger and heavier it became more difficult to move them on roads, and in the muddy conditions of the battlefield. Railway mounted guns began to appear on both sides of the conflict. Special gun mountings and trucks for this super heavy artillery could not be made overnight, crews had to be trained to work them and railway tracks in France altered or strengthened to take them. The number that eventually went into action was insignificant when compared to the quantity of field guns on the Western Front. Possibly this is why there are few reports of their influence on the outcome of battles. Only thirteen heavy gun and howitzer mounted railway batteries went to France in the First World War. There were usually two guns to each battery. Their firing position was often several miles in the rear so they could not be easily overrun in an enemy advance. Even so it was difficult to move them about quickly. The purpose of the railway guns was to bombard trench fortifications, strong points and bunkers. Heavy railway howitzer batteries bombarded supply dumps, assembly points and road and rail junctions far behind the enemy lines in preparation for an advance. The units in France were:

Railway gun batteries: 18th, 45th, 53rd and 92nd.
Railway howitzer batteries: 44th, 52nd, 63rd, 64th, 82nd, 83rd, 86th, 89th and 128th.

Dr Henry Owens who served on the Western Front gives one of the few graphic descriptions of what it was like to be in the vicinity of a 12-inch railway howitzer when it fired. He was in an assembly trench, which ran across a field of oats near the town of Albert. Walking up the railway line towards Dernancourt he said, 'I watched as an enormous shell about 6 feet long was shoved into the barrel, then two or three packets of cordite, then they kicked up the barrel to 45 degrees. When it fired the whole thing seemed wrapped around in flame and a hot blast hit you with a bang, which was quite painful. The whole truck slid about 15 yards up the line.'

Railway mounted guns and howitzers began to be used operationally from late 1915 onwards when the Western Front settled down to static warfare with permanent lines of trenches and blockhouses facing each side, protected by thickets of barbed wire. Reports in the Imperial War Museum confirm that railway guns were in action on the Western Front at Maricouf and Camires in 1916, at Boesinghe and Ypres in 1917 and at Lovez a year later.

It is perhaps not surprising that railway guns only get a brief mention in the histories of the First World War. Their slow rate of fire against distant unseen targets up to 20 miles away lacked the immediacy of front-line action. Gun barrels quickly wore out and had to be replaced or firing them became less accurate. Changing the barrels took time, as did moving such heavy ordnance to a new position. An Operation Order issued by General Rawlinson in 1915 lists the artillery to carry out a bombardment in support of an attack by the 1st, 15th and 47th infantry divisions. Eighty-five field guns supported the attack but only two 9.2-inch railway mounted guns took part.

In his diaries, Lord Crawford, serving in the ranks as a private at a casualty clearing station in France, remembers a conversation he had with a locomotive driver of a railway gun train. He was told that a siege gun on a special truck with sixteen pairs of wheels took two days to travel from the coast to the trenches, stopping six times as its weight kept breaking the rails. (A 14-inch gun and carriage weighed about 164 tons.) A special train had to follow it with a train crew to raise it when it came off the rails. Railway tunnels were also a problem and often the gun barrel had to be removed from its mounting to get it through.

When the war ended ordnance records show that 107 heavy guns were reported as still serviceable, although it is not known how many were railway mounted equipment.

Twelve British railway companies loaned or sold locomotives to the War Office for service in France. The Great Western Railway (GWR) sent a batch of Dean Goods 0-6-0 engines, very reliable and suitable for new drivers of railway gun trains. Rail-mounted artillery and thirty-two engines are known to have been shipped across the Channel to France from the specially built military port of Richborough in Kent. When an unknown number of railway gun trains were returned to Britain at the end of the war they went into Government ordnance depots and were largely forgotten. Their mountings and carriages were dismantled and the gun barrels either scrapped or stored.

After the First World War

In the 1930s the Army Council met to review and decide what its artillery needs would be in any future war. Inevitably this took account of their experiences in the First World War and for railway guns their cost and performance was compared to other artillery. They were well aware of the accuracy and greater shelling power of heavy guns and howitzers, but knew too that their barrels had a shorter life and it took much longer to bring them into action. The Committee was also doubtful whether a future war would become bogged down in trenches as mechanisation was pointing the way to greater mobility in warfare. The cost of developing better railway guns and carriages was also high and so they left the matter in abeyance and did not recommend any more being built. With hindsight their decision was correct. At that time nations were disarming and money was very tight. Any available finance (and there was not much) was being given to newer artillery needs, and modernising medium anti-tank and anti-aircraft guns.

Government production statistics for 9.2-inch and 12-inch artillery built in Britain are obscure and incomplete. There had been no new designs since 1917, only modifications and some changes to mounts and gun barrels. The 12-inch Marks 3 and 5 howitzers (First World War) remained on active service until the 1940s, as did the 9.2 Mark 13 gun. Both were fitted onto specially built railway trucks, some being manufactured in the London, Midland and Scottish (LMS) engineering works at Derby. These were the principal railway guns used for anti-invasion defence in the Second World War, most being in Kent and Sussex.

A railway counter-bombardment battery of British 12-inch howitzers in action in France during the First World War. (**R A Library Picture**)

BL 12-inch railway howitzer Mark 5 on truck Mark 3. This last design by Elswick Co, firing broadside from the railway line, was very successful. It was in service from 1917 until the Second World War. **(Firepower – The Royal Artillery Museum)**

Unloading howitzer shells from a French truck into a wagon taking them to the battery.

A gun crew at rest on their railway gun.

This 12-inch Mark 5 howitzer battery was hidden in a wood near Lovez, France, in 1918.

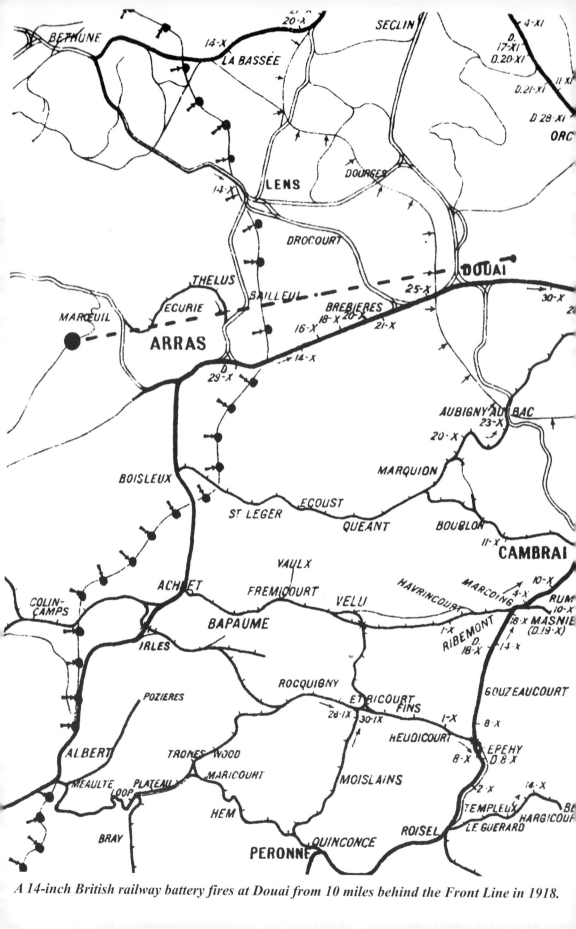

A 14-inch British railway battery fires at Douai from 10 miles behind the Front Line in 1918.

A 12-inch railway howitzer with its gun barrel closed down for travelling.
(R A Library Picture)

A 9.2-inch Mark 3 railway gun at Marincourt in 1917. At this date, gunners were not issued with steel helmets.

A 12-inch Mark 9 railway gun on a truck Mark 2 in France during the First World War, manned by 53 siege battery RA. It has a range of 18 miles.

An exploded view of a 9.2-inch gun on its 12-wheel bogie railway truck.

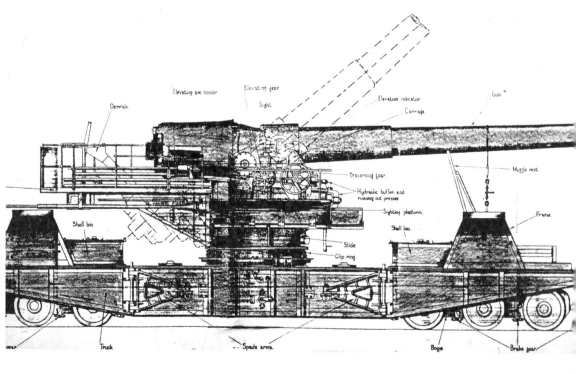

British BL 9.2-inch Mark 13 railway gun in action in France, c.1917–1918. Camouflage netting can be seen covering most of the gun's carriage, the railway wagon and ammunition supply.

A diagram showing the right elevation of British BL 9.2-inch Mark 10 gun, on railway mounting Mark 3 and railway truck Mark 2 (straight back truck) during the First World War.

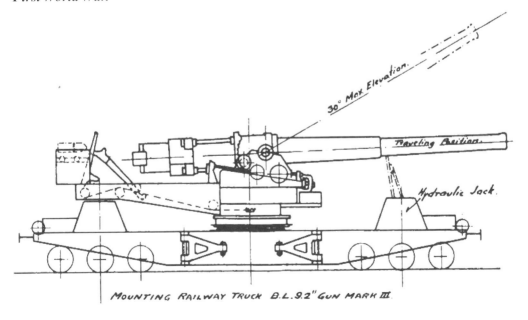

British BL 9.2-inch Mark 13 railway gun, c.1917–1918.

A heavy railway gun, which has just finished firing a round and is about to be covered up.

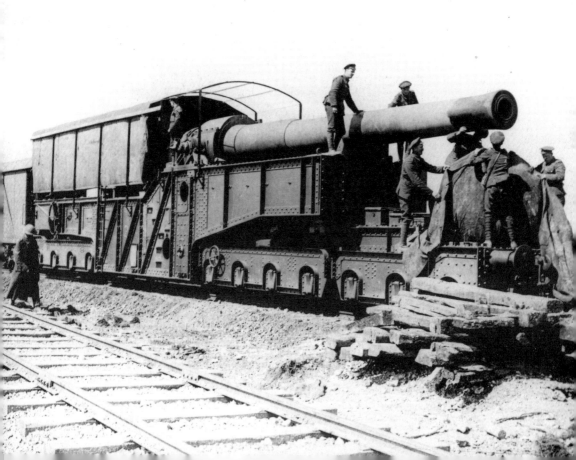

14-inch rail-mounted Armstrong Whitworth BL gun, Mark 3.
(National Army Museum)

The Maharaja of Patiala inspects a heavy railway gun near Bonne, France.
(National Army Museum)

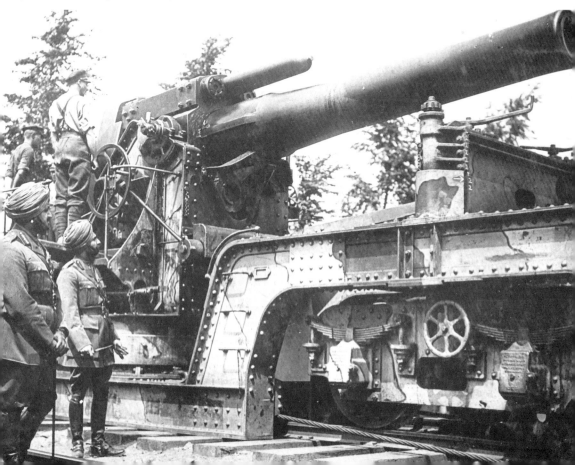

North Eastern Railway 0-6-0 tender goods 2338, later LNER Class J27, in works grey, c.1914. These locomotives were used to haul and position heavy railway guns in Britain and on the Western Front in the First World War. (John Scott-Morgan Collection)

BL 12-inch railway howitzer Mark 3, built by Elswick Co in 1916, mounted on a well base Mark 2 truck. The crew are sponging out the gun barrel after firing. **(Firepower – The Royal Artillery Museum)**

BL 12-inch howitzer Mark 3, preparing to fire as gunners check the percussion fuses on the 750-pound shells. (Firepower – The Royal Artillery Museum)

A BL 14-inch gun named Scene Shifter is ready to fire. One of the two built by Elswick Co, it was in service near Etaples, France, with 471 Battery, RGA, in 1918. (Firepower – The Royal Artillery Museum)

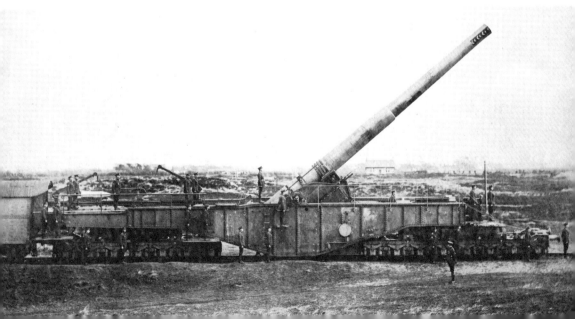

BL 9.2-inch Mark 10 railway gun on the truck Mark 2, in service from August 1916 until the Second World War. It is seen here at Elswick Co works with two civilians. (Firepower – The Royal Artillery Museum)

Rear view of the BL 12-inch railway howitzer Mark 5, on truck Mark 3. This final design from Elswick Co was in service from 1917 until the Second World War. (Firepower – The Royal Artillery Museum)

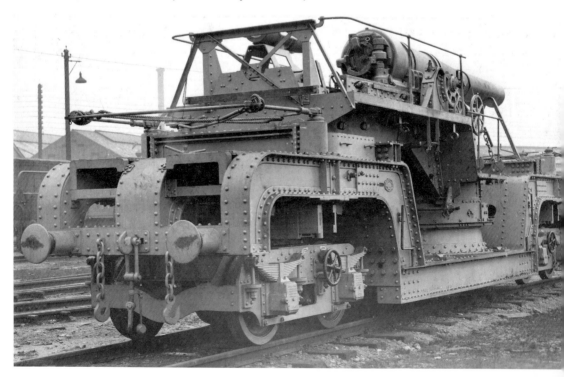

BL 12-inch Mark 1 railway howitzer on truck Mark 1, built by Elswick Co. Its steep trajectory demolished trenches and other defences. It was in service from 1916.
(Firepower – The Royal Artillery Museum)

The first British 9.2-inch railway gun on truck Mark 1, built by Elswick Co in 1915. When fired, the gun recoiled on a Vasseur slide mounting.
(Firepower – The Royal Artillery Museum)

BL 12-inch Mark 5 showing the long loading platform needed to balance the gun and facilitate the loading of shells, each weighing 750 pounds. **(Firepower – The Royal Artillery Museum)**

BL 12-inch Mark 5. Restraining steel cables kept the gun steady at every angle when it fired and were fixed into the ground with iron spades.
(Firepower – The Royal Artillery Museum)

BL 12-inch Mark 5 railway howitzer, shown here in travelling mode with poles for camouflage netting folded down. (Firepower – The Royal Artillery Museum)

BL 12-inch Mark 5 showing the well-bed, which is supporting the central pivot for the gun, and the two 4-wheel bogies of railway truck Mark 3. (Firepower – The Royal Artillery Museum)

BL 12-inch railway gun Mark 9 in truck Mark 1 with gun raised in the firing position. Designed by Vickers, the gun was in service in France in 1915 but defects resulted in modifications. (Firepower – The Royal Artillery Museum)

Chapter 3

American, French and German Railway Guns in the First World War

American railway guns

The Americans had one of the earliest experiences of railway mounted guns in combat. This arose from a suggestion made or at least supported by General Lee of the Confederate Army. He asked the navy to provide him with 'heavy gun on a truck covered in iron' to travel on the Richmond and York River Railway during one of the Seven Days Battles of the American Civil War. In June 1862 this battery was ordered to advance and open fire. It moved, propelled by steam down the track, passed into a deep cut, opened fire with its 32-pound gun and sent a shell beyond the first line of the Federals and over the heads of their reserves forcing them to shift their position.

Although the Americans were aware that railway artillery was being developed in other countries, there was little call for it at home until war broke out in 1914, when they realised they had none of their own design. When they entered the European war in April 1916, they had already commenced preliminary discussions to fill this gap. Five, 14-inch/50-calibre railway guns, mountings and locomotives were ordered for the American Navy in November 1917 from the Baldwin Locomotive Works of Pennsylvania. These were delivered the following Spring. Some equipment came from the Standard Steel Company. The design of the mountings was such as to enable them to pass over bridges and through tunnels safely in France.

General Pershing, who was commanding the 1st American Army on the Western Front, wanted them shipped to the port of St Nazaire to avoid capture or destruction by the enemy who had installed a number of railway guns on concrete bases along the Belgian coast. Each gun was designated a single battery and five arrived in France on 10 June 1918. Batteries 1 and 2 were loaned to support the French Army, and 3, 4 and 5 were deployed around Verdun on the Western Front. Crewed by sailors, the batteries were under the command of Rear Admiral Plunkett of the United States Navy.

Each railway battery was made up of a US Army military 2-8-0 locomotive, armoured ammunition wagons, medical and workshop equipment cars, and accommodation and catering carriages. The gun barrels came from surplus ships or naval reserves.

Railway guns were expensive and used sparingly to fire at railway junctions, troop concentrations and storage depots often far behind the German front lines. General Pershing used them to support his offensive in the Meuse-Argonne sector of the Western Front, which began on 25 September 1918. As his offensive was backed with 2,700 pieces of artillery, which included only a handful of railway guns, their contribution to the advance was useful but only minimal. Two of the guns fired upon the railway line that ran from Sedan and beyond Metz, which was then an important rail communications centre. Three guns in the eastern sector of the battlefield were aimed at German forces around St Quentin.

The life of a railway gun barrel was calculated at about 300 shells fired and as each gun fired about half this number, and as the Armistice was signed forty-eight days later, it seems they must have stood idle for a time during the final battle.

The 14-inch American railway guns were the only ones to arrive in France and see action before the Armistice. It was intended to send a batch of 8-inch railway guns from America to France, but only three arrived as the war ended.

The gun carriage of the American 14-inch (50cm) Mark 4 Railway gun was built of steel plates over two longitudinal girders, mounted on four six-wheel bogies. Its maximum range was 23 miles, and it fired a shell weighing 1,400 pounds (640kg). It could traverse only 2.5 degrees left or right of the centre rail track. For a greater traverse, a curved track (epis) had to be specially laid. To reduce the strain of the recoil on the gun car, it was necessary to dig a pit 9 feet (2.7m) deep in which brackets could be buried to transmit recoil energy into the earth.

The actual achievements of the five American railway guns that went to France in the First World War are buried in their War Diaries. One important contribution they are said to have made is the destruction of a German supply dump near Laon, as well as the cutting of the railway line in several places already mentioned.

French railway guns

France entered the First World War with a sufficiency of field guns but a shortage of heavy guns, perhaps half of which were obsolete, dating from the nineteenth century. Design and development in this area had suffered from lack of political interest and investment. Of all the combatants France had the largest stock of railway guns and at the end of the war this was estimated to be about 400 out of an artillery stock of 7,000. Many of the early railway guns dated from the late nineteenth century and as the war continued these were replaced by newer models, which were built or adapted by the French armament firm, Schneider. It was often easier to remove surplus gun barrels from naval ships or stores, and remount them onto platforms on railway trucks before transfer to land service with the army. Between 1914 and 1918 there were six main types of French railway gun in addition to others remaining from previous wars. Some of these could not be traversed from the centre line and had to be aimed directly at the target, but with their gun barrels raised 40–60 degrees they could fire over distances of up to 16 to 28 miles. To overcome the disadvantage of a limited traverse the French laid down curved spurs from the main line. These were known as 'epis' or 'firing tracks' and enabled the gun train to be positioned to fire in a spread of directions.

The later French guns, because of their weight, were usually mounted on a heavy box structure resting on two or more four-wheel bogies. The fixings mounting the barrel onto the carriage varied – sliding, rolling and pedestal. Where the smaller guns could be traversed 360 degrees there were two outriggers each side to keep it steady. As with railway guns everywhere the gun and carriage were heavy structures. The heaviest was *Obusier de 520*, a howitzer weighing 290 tons (260,000kg). Two of these were almost ready in 1918, but one blew up with a shell in the breech. It had a range of 105 miles, but its rate of fire was one shell every six minutes. The war ended before it was operational.

There was usually one railway locomotive for each gun train. A reserve park of gun barrels, cranes, locomotives and engineering workshops was set up many miles behind the Front Line to service French rail artillery.

German railway guns

In the twentieth century Germany had an efficient network of railways, which extended across its land borders to connect with those of neighbouring countries. In war the railway was essential to move troops and supplies, especially heavy artillery. The early German railway guns were better engineered but little different in conception from those used during the American Civil War and the Siege of Paris a few years later. They were wheeled field guns put on top of a railway wagon. Because they could be fired mounted or dismounted they were also known as railway road guns.

When Germany went to war in 1914, they expected a short war by overcoming the French Army and capturing Paris. If this was possible it was not to be, for they were stopped in September at the Battle of the Marne and the result was the creation of the Western Front, 400 miles long, stretching from the English Channel to Switzerland. Both armies dug in behind extensive trench systems and shelled each other day and night for the rest of the war, gaining and losing ground from time to time. Guns and howitzers fired at front-line troops, but there was soon a demand for heavier weapons to destroy strong fortifications, magazines and supply dumps behind the trenches. The German arms firm, Krupps, was asked for artillery with greater firepower, which for strategic reasons needed to be mobile. Moving such heavy weapons by horses or tractors was impractical so the solution was to put them on strengthened railway trucks. For various reasons the German Navy had a surplus of gun barrels, and Krupps were asked to design mountings to which these could be fitted. This posed a new set of problems, which had to be resolved – recoil, stability and the degree to which the gun could be traversed from the centre of the railway line. Krupp's solved these difficulties with German ingenuity and thoroughness, but it was not until the last two years of the war that they were ready for action.

Compared to the number of field guns the Germans had on the Western Front, their few railway guns did not amount to much extra firepower. It is possible that less than 120 German railway mounted gun trains were built and equipped, and not all would have been continually in operation. Complicated pieces of machinery needed maintenance, and when a railway gun was moved to a new site it took several days.

As with the railway guns of the Allies, the German railway guns had little effect on the outcome of a battle or the course of the war. Organised in batteries of two guns each, the Germans usually deployed them singly, serving in a support role to cause destruction in rear areas, or as siege guns to batter strong enemy positions. Operationally, they had disadvantages. Their rate of fire was limited to perhaps not much more than one round every few minutes. Like the French they relied upon aerial observation aeroplanes or balloons for reliable information about the fall of shot. Although they could move about freely miles behind the lines, it often took several days to get them into position. The 21cm SK gun, nicknamed 'Peter Adalbert', was mounted on a central pivot and needed to be assembled by a crane, which took up to five days. Some railway guns with very heavy gun barrels held in place by trunions could not be traversed more than a degree or so, and spur lines had to be laid so that they could be aligned with the target.

German railway guns had a range of 10–17 miles, depending upon the model, and fired explosive or armour piercing shells weighing up to 300 pounds (136kg). The 38cm SK L/45 'Max', which took part in the Spring Offensive in 1918, had a range of 27 miles.

German rail gun equipment on the Western Front was distributed to army corps on the basis of the importance of the target to be destroyed behind the lines. Moving them about on the rail network was not easy because of their weight, and some needed pits or platforms prepared so that their barrels could be fully elevated. About eight different types of German rail guns were in use during the war.

The calibre (the internal diameter of the gun barrel), degree of elevation, traverse, muzzle velocity depending on the charge, and weight of shell governed the distance a gun could fire. The 28cm KL/40 had a range of 17 miles, whereas the larger SK L/45 was able to fire up to 27 miles. The larger bore guns did not arrive on the battlefield before 1917, about the same time as other combatants were investing in heavier guns. Although their operational history is sketchy, German rail guns (21cm 'Peter Adalbert') took part at Verdun in 1916 and at Passchendaele in 1917. The 24cm 'Theodor Karl' was used on the Somme in 1916, and the heavier rail gun 38cm 'Max', with others, took part in the German Spring Offensive of 1918. German railway guns came mostly from obsolete ships or naval armouries and might be crewed by naval or army gunners depending upon whether they had been handed over to the army. Rail guns with SK in the title were from ships.

Between the end of the war and 1920, Col. H.W. Miller of the United States Ordnance Department wrote a series of reports evaluating the construction and performance of railway guns on the Western Front. His comprehensive report ran to over 800 pages, complete with illustrations, engineering drawings and performance statistics. Generally Col. Miller seems to have been impressed with German railway artillery and the mechanisms designed to elevate and traverse the gun and control its recoil when fired. He found the 15cm SK 'Nathan' of sturdy construction, but its limited 26-degree traverse was a serious disadvantage, possibly because it was on a mounting which had been improvised. The 21cm SK L/40 'Peter Adalbert' had a steel firing platform which took seven rail cars to transport and three to five days to set up, and needed a crane for the job. Some of the other gun trains he noted suffered the same disadvantage, but the elevation and traversing actions on the 21cm guns were good. At the end of the war the railway guns were either destroyed or confiscated and given to other governments.

German long-range gun (the Paris gun)

The Paris Gun was famous, because its performance broke new ground in artillery construction. It was perhaps not a truly mobile railway gun as its weight and size meant it was moved in sections and assembled at its firing site. Even so, for a one-off artillery development, it was far ahead of its time and its manufacture was kept secret from the Allies. This was a very long-range gun designed and successfully built by the Krupp's armament firm. It must have been under construction for some time because there were many technical problems to solve and it was not ready until March 1918, a few months before the end of the war.

At this time Paris was almost 80 miles (131km) behind the Front Line. When the city awoke to unexplained explosions, there was a lot of alarm and panic. Examination of fragments revealed that they came from an artillery shell and the hunt was on to seek out the gun site, which was later found to be in the Forest of

Gohain, west of Laon. It was not until after the war that it was found out that the Germans had built seven special long-range guns with barrels extended to a length of 118 feet (34 metres), based on their 38 SK L/45 naval gun. Mounted on a cradle between trunnions on a rail-car body of girders, connected by steel transoms to steel trucks with four and five axle bogies, it could only move slowly. A gantry crane was needed to help in its installation.

Aside from the initial panic the bombardment caused by shells landing on Paris, their actual destructive power was poor. Between March and August 1918 over 300 shells of 264 pounds (120kg) were fired, causing some loss of life and property damage. It was reckoned that despite the effect on civilian morale, it was no worse than an air raid and hardly justified the resources put into the project.

The French and British governments were developing similar long-range guns, but Germany was the first in 1918 to operate a railway gun whose shells reached this distance. 25 miles (40km) above the earth, shells traveled the 76 miles (121km) to Paris in 170 seconds. The wear on the gun barrels, which needed changing after twenty shells fired, and the visible damage caused, made the project uneconomical. To the ingenuity of the design of this artillery piece a certain mystery was added. All the guns were removed by the Germans and destroyed before the Allies could make a proper evaluation of them, and few of the German officials involved in the project would talk about its operation.

American workers and gunners on a Naval 14-inch, 50-calibre railway gun in France in 1918. The locomotive is on the left.

A muzzle-loading 32-pounder naval gun, mounted on a crude railway platform. It was designed by John Mercer Brooke and served by Confederate gunners in the American Civil war.

A restored locomotive, one of 1,500 built by Baldwin's for General Pershing's campaign in France in 1916–1918. Drawbar tractive effort 35,400 pounds.

American troops built this camouflaged emplacement for a 340mm French railway gun in France in 1917.

French gunners rest on their 274mm railway mounted gun on the Western Front in 1916.

An early French railway mortar being camouflaged under trees in 1917.

Two early (1915) French Material 320 railway guns in a siding near the Western Front.

The crew, locomotive and 28cm German railway gun ('Bruno') along with its coaches, were captured near Harbonnières in August 1918.

German War Department steam locomotive No. 454 with officers at the Front during the First World War.

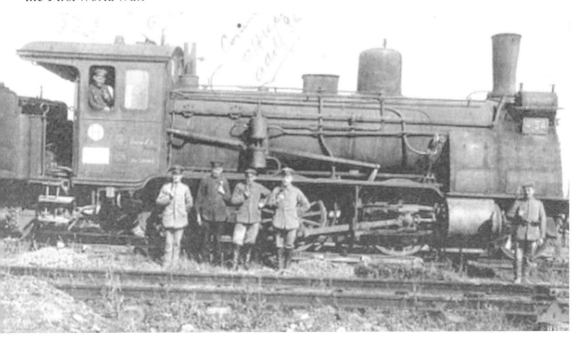

The Paris gun with struts necessary to brace its drooping barrel, which was 112 feet (34 metres) long. It weighed 256 tons. Mounted on a railway truck for transport, it had to be emplaced in concrete with a turntable before being fired.

Track layout with firing positions for railway guns on the edge of a wood. Spurs (epis) curve off to give different traverse options. (Col. Miller)

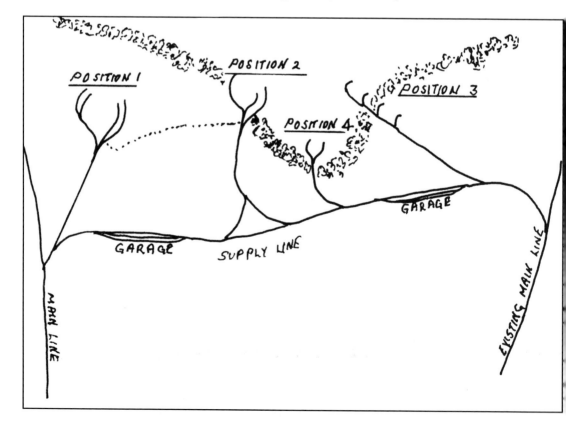

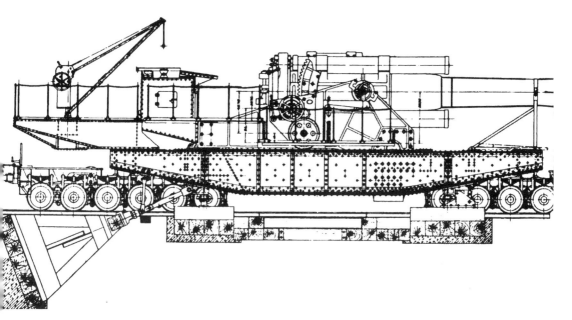

Method of anchoring a railway truck into the ground so that it holds firm when the gun fires and recoils on its slide.

The US Navy 14-inch railway gun, which was in action on the Western Front in 1918.

Captured German heavy railway guns. (National Army Museum)

The 14-inch, 50-calibre railway guns were spare US Navy Mark 4 14-inch, 50-calibre guns, mounted on railway cars and operated by US Navy crews in France in the closing months of the First World War. Photograph of US 14-inch railway gun firing in Thierville-sur-Meuse, France, in 1918.

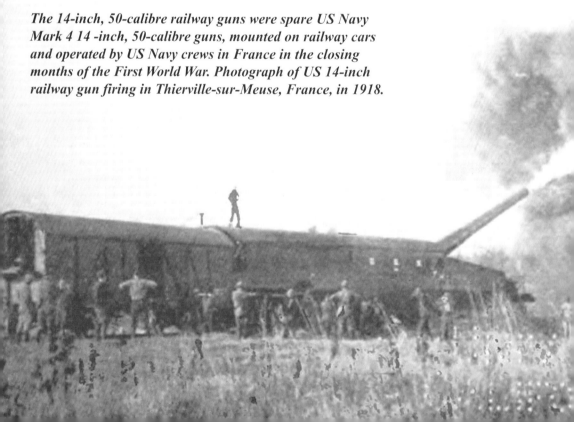

Chapter 4

Gunners and Sappers

The Royal Regiment of Artillery (the Gunners)

Before the First World War the Royal Regiment of Artillery had three quite separate branches – Horse, Field, and Garrison. The first two gave mobile, light and medium gun support to the cavalry and infantry divisions of the field army. The Garrison artillery manned static guns in border and coastal forts and supported the field army with siege guns firing from fixed positions. The distinction between the three branches became less relevant after 1915 when more use began to be made of much heavier guns.

When war on the Western Front in France settled down into permanent trench warfare the destruction of supplies and communications in the enemy's rear led to both sides designing and using long-range guns and howitzers firing at targets out of sight. Horses and tractors pulled most of the artillery, but the heaviest guns, some with their ammunition weighing 200 tons or more, could only be moved successfully on the railway. Special well-bed or flatbed trucks with many sets of bogies and special platforms were built on which these very heavy guns and howitzers could be mounted and traversed. Thus of necessity close cooperation developed between gunners of the Royal Artillery and sappers from the Royal Engineers who laid down the railway spurs and drove and maintained the engines which pulled the guns into position.

Siege gun training

A practice school for siege gun training was opened at Lydd on the Kent coast from about 1882 up to and during the First World War. It was also used for various ordnance experiments. In 1916 its sole battery of guns was said to be muzzle-loaders and howitzers left over from the Boer War, so practical training with heavy siege artillery was limited. Although the Lydd camp and its ranges were connected by a branch line to the main South Eastern Railway line at Appledore there is no record that railway guns used it during the First World War and certainly not afterwards as in 1921 the school was moved to Larkhill on Salisbury Plain where it was amalgamated with the School of Artillery. From all accounts because of financial constraints, apart from lectures, practical training in working railway artillery was not undertaken.

In 1939 it was decided to restart a training programme for 9.2-inch and 12-inch guns and howitzers on railway mountings. Training was to be at Larkhill camp as the Westdown and Tilshead artillery ranges could accommodate long distance shelling. Even this did not happen because a few months later it was decided that it would be better to move the training school to Catterick near Richmond in Yorkshire. Catterick garrison and its ranges covered an area of 25 square miles. Major, (later Colonel) S.M. Cleeve who had commanded a battery of railway guns in 1918 was asked by the War Office to put his past experience to good use and organise a number of new railway batteries and train their crews how to use them. An innovative artillery officer he searched ordnance depots for guns and mountings, which he was aware had been kept and stored after the First World War. After training had been completed gun crews were sent from Catterick to the Salisbury Plain ranges and the artillery school at Okehampton in Devon where Dartmoor was used for practice shoots.

Royal Engineers (sappers)

The War Department's association with railways began as far back as 1865 with the appointment of an advisory group to co-ordinate the use of railways for military and civilian purposes in an emergency. A small branch of the Royal Engineers with responsibility for railway working had been established even earlier, brought about by campaigns overseas in the Crimea, Middle East and Africa.

Training railway sappers

It was not until after 1905 that land at Longmoor on the Surrey – Hampshire border was bought and developed as a permanent railway training centre for the British Army. It seems that for several years more attention was paid to training men in railway construction and less to working and maintaining locomotives. In 1908 Longmoor was renamed the Woolmer Instructional Railway and in the First World War its camps, tracks and shunting yards were expanded to include the area around Whitehill and Bordon. These places were connected by about 70 miles of railway lines on which War Department-acquired locomotives were used to train recruits in driving, shunting, signalling and engine maintenance. During the First World War locomotives in the military service were marked ROD (Railway Operating Division) and numbered. By 1918 over 26,000 sappers had been trained at Longmoor in all branches of railway construction and train operating.

During the peace of the 1920–30s Government economies left the Longmoor military railway system in a rundown state. On the outbreak of the Second World War it was expanded to cope with an influx of conscripted men. Many came directly from their civilian job in the railway companies. Ranked as sappers they underwent a basic 8-week course in army discipline, drill and weapon training.

Job training in military railway operating and maintenance followed. By 1945 more than 58,000 had passed through the Longmoor camps. Three months into the war the Longmoor facilities were found to be insufficient to handle all the new recruits and No 2 Training Centre was opened in Derby. Close by was the Traffic School of the London, Midland and Scottish Railway Company (LMS) which made its workshops available for training in the different railway trades; drivers, firemen, fitters and blocksmen (signallers). An 11-mile-long railway line from junctions near Ashby-de-la-Zouch (Leicestershire) and Charleston East (Derbyshire) came into use as the Melbourne Military Railway, this being the principal station on the line. It was used for practice in railway operating and track maintenance.

When their technical training was completed sappers were classified as tradesmen according to a strict hierarchy of skills and paid accordingly. Thus drivers of steam locomotives were graded 'A', diesel drivers 'B', shunters 'C', fitters 'E' and so on. The men were then posted to railway operating, workshop, bridging and construction companies attached to Army Groups and Divisions.

Organisation in the field

Each Army Division was able to call on specialised Royal Engineer companies with the technical ability and skills to undertake the construction, operation and maintenance of the railway system in its area. The officers and sappers in these companies included tradesmen to drive and service locomotives, and to ensure tracks, bridges and tunnels were properly strengthened to carry heavy loads such as railway mounted guns. Officers from the Royal Artillery advised where extra lines, sidings and spurs were needed and curves improved so that railway guns could be placed in the best firing positions. In Britain the railway companies co-operated in closing stations and lines to civilian use so that priority was given to the defence of the area.

Movement of railway guns

The movement of the cumbersome railway guns from one location to another usually took place at night and avoided London as much as possible because of air raids and disruption. Routes were a closely guarded secret as were all military movements at the time. There was a great fear of spies and fifth columnists that might pass information to the enemy. The suppression of news about what was going on led to rumours, which fuelled these fears. The movement of railway guns from the Kent coast to Devon for training purposes meant a journey via Tunbridge Wells, Basingstoke, Andover and Salisbury. At Okehampton there were extensive artillery ranges and rail-mounted 9.2-inch howitzers fired onto Dartmoor from sidings near the Asbury and Halwill junctions on the branch line to Bude. In

Wiltshire on Salisbury Plain 18- and 9.2-inch howitzers took part in exercises with XII Corps in preparation for the D-Day landings. The guns fired from outside the range boundaries, the former from the Bulford branch line and the 9.2-inch from the main line at Porton.

The railway mounted gun on its special truck, cordite van, stores van, officers' and sergeants' coaches, galley, mess wagon, accommodation coaches for gunners and a brake van formed a lengthy train clanking its way through the night drawn by a steam train or perhaps two diesel locomotives. Journeys might take several days if it was left in sidings to allow more pressing military traffic to pass. The greatest danger to its safety in daylight came from low-level air raids if it was travelling near the coast.

Royal Field Artillery.

Royal Horse Artillery.

Royal Garrison Artillery.

40/W.O./6049.

FOR OFFICIAL USE ONLY.
This Document is the property of H.B.M. Government, and the information in it is not to be communicated, either directly or indirectly, to the Press or any person not holding an official position in His Majesty's Service.

TRAINING INSTRUCTIONS

FOR

SIEGE ARTILLERY.

To supersede 40/W.O./4402.

ISSUED BY THE GENERAL STAFF,

JULY, 1918.

PRINTED UNDER AUTHORITY OF H.M. STATIONERY OFFICE,
BY KING & JARRETT, LTD., BLACKFRIARS, LONDON, S.E. 1.

Wt. W6190/PP1461 14m 3/18 K&J 2313 Misc.2.

Instructions for siege artillery in 1918, which were still current in the Second World War.

he Ordnance BL 12-inch collection of British rmy railway howitzers developed for siege perations of the First World War.

A Class J27 0-6-0 locomotive was used to move heavy railway mounted guns on the Catterick Camp military railway. (**Author's Collection**)

Gun crews for 9.2-inch railway guns under training in Northern Command in 1941.

A rare picture of a 12-inch railway gun under trees with its camouflaged netting in place.

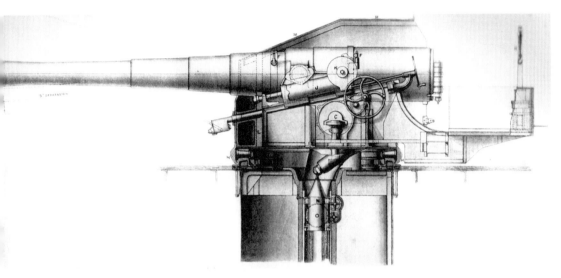

A 9.2-inch Vavasseur centre pivot mounting Mark 3 used for some railway guns and howitzers.

Diagram of British 12-inch Mark 5 high-explosive artillery shell, for BL 12-inch howitzer and BL 12-inch railway howitzer. 1917. (**Author's Collection**)

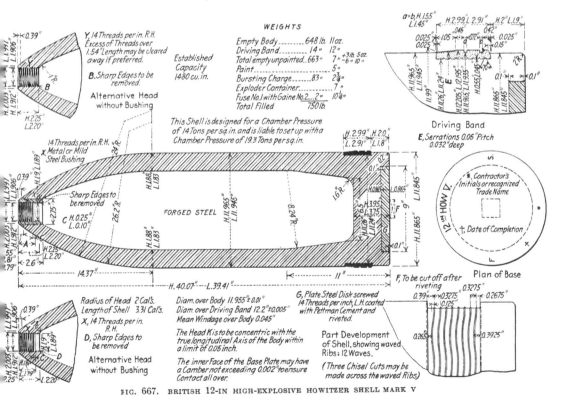

FIG. 667.   BRITISH 12-IN HIGH-EXPLOSIVE HOWITZER SHELL MARK V

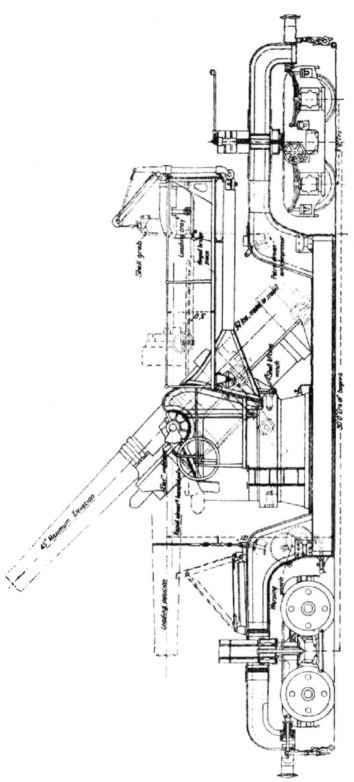

12-INCH HOWITZER MARK III AND V. CAR LOWERED ON TO BEAMS FOR FIRING.

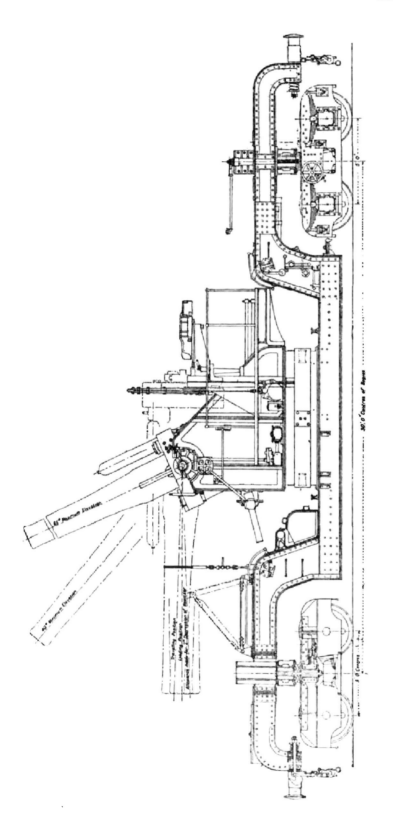

British 12-inch howitzer shown in firing and travelling position

Crew and British BL 18-inch railway howitzer at Ashbury Station prior to firing into Oakhampton Artillery Range.

14-inch railway gun at Dover.

18-inch howitzer on railway mounting. (Top) in action. (Middle) in travelling mode. The metal frames under the muzzle are for 'bulking out' the tarpaulin cover to disguise it from aircraft when on the move

The US 8-inch railway gun Mk6 M3A2, on mount M1A1.

A 9.2-inch railway gun, Mark 13, being fired in Britain in 1940.

A 12-inch Mark 3 railway howitzer in France, 1939.

The BL 14-inch railway gun, named 'Boche Buster', on truck Mark 1 is closed down for travelling. Weighing 248 tons, it had a range of 21 miles. (Firepower – The Royal Artillery Museum)

The 14-inch railway gun Scene Shifter with gunners and four artillery officers. The chalk inscription on the van reads 'keep off the gun' (Firepower – The Royal Artillery Museum)

Chapter 5

The Return of Railway Guns in 1940

At the start of the Second World War in 1939 the British Expeditionary Force (BEF) went to France insufficiently and poorly equipped. Its order of battle was broadly based on what had been needed in 1918. It was recognised that most of its artillery was obsolete, economies having stifled development. With the BEF went the 52nd Super Heavy Regiment. Its artillery is known to have included 6-inch, 8-inch and 9.2-inch howitzers, an unknown number of which were mounted on railway trucks. How many of this unknown number survived destruction or capture to return to this country after Dunkirk is uncertain, but the regiment is known to have lost fifty-four of its heavy guns.

A War Office report later confirmed the BEF had left nearly *all* its artillery in the retreat from France, most of it being of First World War vintage. The number involved was said to have been about 933 guns and howitzers of various calibres. Possibly no great disaster in the long term because of their obsolescence, but more worryingly at the time, was news that replacement was expected to take five months. It seems that apart from any guns left in Britain super heavy gun batteries had ceased to exist.

The evacuation of the British Army from the Dunkirk beaches was completed by early June 1940 and a desperate attempt was made to make good its losses to counter an expected German seaborne invasion. The English Channel coast within striking distance of France, (21 miles, 34km, between Dover and Calais) had never been properly fortified with fixed coastal batteries because of the perceived strength of the Royal Navy and the absence of any serious threat since Napoleon in 1803. Thus almost overnight there was a need for any gun heavier than a field gun to be rushed to the coast for the defence of the landing beaches and the destruction of the enemy at sea. This was not the role for which railway siege guns had been intended and indeed they were completely unsuitable. However, Prime Minister Winston Churchill insisted that the number of heavy guns at Dover had to be increased and so action to do this was taken. Colonel S.M. Cleeve, a gunner with big gun battle experience in the First World War, had been promoted Commandant of the School of Super Heavy Artillery at Catterick Camp in Yorkshire. It was here that men were trained to work 9.2-inch, 12-inch and several much larger guns all mounted on railway trucks. The War Office, spurred into action by pressure from the prime minister, ordered Colonel Cleeve to seek out any type of heavy gun which could be used to attack the enemy if he approached the coast. It had been the practice for guns removed from ships to be stored and Colonel Cleeve found some 13.5-inch naval guns in the Ruddington Ordnance Depot on the outskirts of Nottingham. These had come originally from the battleship *Iron Duke* (10 x 13.5-inch guns), which had distinguished itself in the Battle of Jutland, but had been scrapped in the 1930s. Colonel Cleeve also knew of the existence of 14-inch/18-inch railway mountings, which could be converted to fit these old naval guns. The North British locomotive works at Darlington carried out the work. Subsequently they were sent to the Kent coast bearing old First World War nameplates, *Scene Shifter*, *Gladiator* and *Piecemaker*.

Another addition to railway artillery was that of a 14-inch gun, which came from a battleship the *Almirante Cochrane*, built for the Chilean navy in 1916 but never delivered, scrapped in 1926, and the mounting stored. In 1940 it was fitted with an 18-inch barrel. This gun bore the nameplate *Boche Buster* which had been removed from a gun formerly in action in the First World War at Arras when manned by 471 Siege Battery.

Following Churchill's directive another heavy gun, which ended up near Dover, but not until 1942, was a hyper-velocity gun comprising a 13.5-inch barrel with an 8-inch liner. This experimental gun could fire a 256-pound (116kg) shell over 62 miles (99km) and is thought to have been named *Bruce* after the then Controller of the Royal Navy.

Deployment of the Super Heavy railway batteries

By September 1940 thirteen Super Heavy railway batteries of two 9.2-inch or 12-inch howitzers had been assembled into three regiments and allocated to Eastern, Southern and Northern Commands in Britain. A third regiment also had two Super Heavy Batteries called 'X' and 'Y' attached from the Royal Canadian Artillery.

When General Sir Alanbrooke was appointed as Chief of the Imperial General Staff (CIGS) he changed the boundaries of Southern Command, which at that time stretched from the Walsh in Lincolnshire to Portsmouth in Hampshire. In his view the length of this vulnerable coastline, split by the Thames Estuary, was too long and likely to cause all sorts of movement and reinforcement problems in the event of an invasion. He formed a new South Western Command along the South Coast, which led to a redeployment of most railway mounted artillery to Kent and Sussex. During a visit he discussed with others the difficulties of *concentrating* the fire of the super howitzers on the landing beaches, which suggests he was aware of their limitations.

There has to be some guesswork about the total number of railway guns in or near the coast of Southern England in the 1940s. Some moved to different parts of the country when practice firing was undertaken or defence priorities changed. The description of artillery as heavy was also ill-defined although super heavy usually meant railway guns, their calibre ranging from 9.2-inch to 18-inch. Regiments, batteries and their locations changed as defence priorities altered. Most railway batteries were armed with one or two 9.2 inch Mark 13 guns or 12-inch Mark 3 howitzers. As previously mentioned there was also some urgent improvisation involving ex-naval gun barrels and First World War mountings from various sources.

An 18-inch howitzer practises firing towards the English Channel, probably from a cutting on the single-track line near Bourne Park tunnel on the Elham line where it was often hidden.

A batch of new 12-inch Mark 5 howitzers on railway mountings outside the LMS wagon works at Derby during the Second World War.

A 2,500-pound shell being loaded into the breach of a super heavy railway howitzer. (Tank Museum, Dorset)

A 12-inch Mark 3 railway howitzer in a Dorset wood. Camouflage netting is stretched overhead between the trees.

Two 9.2-inch railway howitzers at Bargrove Wood on the Ashford to Folkestone line, ready to fire out to sea over Hythe. Nearby railway cuttings provided cover. **(Author's Collection)**

A sapper carries out maintenance on a gun train.

Chapter 6

Train Working for Railway Guns

On the outbreak of war in 1939 there were about 20,000 steam locomotives in the country, many having been designed and built in the previous century, or with modifications since then. There were also a small number of electric, and diesel locomotives. The rolling stock, carriages, brake vans and wagons amounted to more than a million units. Under the Emergency Powers legislation the Ministry of Transport took over control of eleven private and independent undertakings: Southern Railway (SR); Great Western Railway (GWR); London Midland and Scottish Railway (LMS) and several others of which the East Kent Light Railway (EKLR) and the Kent and East Sussex Light Railway (KESL) are relevant to this book. During the course of the war these private companies met the needs of the War Department for locomotives and wagons. Locomotives built for the Ministry of Supply during the war had restrictions on the design and materials used, and were referred to as 'Austerity' locomotives. Many served in military railways in army camps and ranges. Locomotives transferred from private rail companies for army use were usually given War Department numbers.

Make-up of railway mounted gun trains

The make-up of railway gun trains in 1940 was broadly the same as the siege trains that had gone to France in the First World War. The weight of the gun was the reason for it to be mounted on specially built railway trucks. The rolling stock of the train included an ammunition truck for shells and cordite, and wagons for maintenance fitters and stores. Coaches with bunks and a galley enabled the crews to be self-sufficient in remote locations. Spike Milligan, the post-war actor and musician, told how the railway gun unit he was attached to had a converted carriage for the gunners. Pre-war camping coaches from the London, Midland and Scottish Railwayx (LMS), or converted passenger coaches served this purpose well. Wagons held spade arms, small arms and artillery stores. Railway Regulations insisted that each train had a guard's van. The crew of the train numbered about forty men including the locomotive driver.

The steam locomotive which hauled railway guns was initially the Dean Goods 0-6-0. William Dean of the Great Western Railway (GWR) had designed it in 1883 and it was sometimes referred to as Class 2301. The Dean Goods was a reliable locomotive and with its coal tender was used for working heavy goods trains. As a tank engine it was also good for shunting. Its combination of wheels (0-6-0), three each side, gave it superior adhesion against slipping. Moreover its simple operation and controls made it suitable for inexperienced drivers. Engines known to have served in the Kent area had WD numbers 94/5/8/9/100/56/67–72/9/80/95–7. Other locomotives used for pulling 12-inch railway howitzers were the F4s; numbers 1031, 1110 and 1215, with a 2-4-2 wheel arrangement. They were built in 1884 for the Great Eastern Railway, now the London North Eastern Railway (LNER). There were also some J27s (0-6-0) engines built in 1906 for the North Eastern Railway. Although serviceable, like the guns they were getting on in years.

Eventually Armstrong Whitworth diesel electric locomotives 0-6-0 350hp C type, with a jackstaff drive, arrived from the London Midland and Scottish (LMS) railway to replace steam locomotives, which gave away their position with steam and smoke to aircraft. They were numbered 7059, 7061–2, 7063 and 7064. Other diesels built by the English Electric Company in Brighton in their Southern Railways (SR) workshops were also used. Where gradients were steep diesels were needed at both ends of the train to push and pull.

The guns were specially mounted on railway flatbed or well-bed trucks, which allowed high gun platforms to pass through tunnels easily. The wheel arrangement of the truck varied according to the weight and length of the gun barrel. A 9.2-inch calibre gun stood on a truck with two 6-wheel bogies while the 18-inch gun had 8-wheel and 6-wheel bogies in front, and 8-wheel and 6-wheel bogies at the rear.

When the gun was pushed or pulled to the firing site the rest of the train was parked further down the line under trees or in sidings. In areas where railway guns were operating the line was taken over by the army and closed to public use.

Army engineers often had to make changes to the track layout so that railway gun trains could move about freely. A single line was needed at Ashford to connect with Canterbury West and another from Faversham to the line at Canterbury East. Previously little-used lines also needed to have extra ballast laid, and some curves were made less severe to take these heavy trains and minimise the shock waves when the guns were fired.

Train working

In the War Office instruction manual, *Railways*, locomotive drivers were told that the tractive force (or effort) exerted by a locomotive to overcome resistance and push a heavy load could be explained by a mathematical formula, but that this was too complicated for practical working. It went on to say that there were many different opinions as to the amount of pull or push (known as drawbar pull) needed to start an engine and then keep it moving. Boiler size and efficiency, fuel quality, lubricants, train weight, adhesion and gradients were all likely to affect performance. Also it was not possible to compare the tractive effort of different locomotives, as this was a measure of ability to start a train and not the ability to haul it. Drivers were told that a practical test of how a locomotive performed was better than theoretical deductions and they should try out their engines to get the best results. This was the best practical advice in the circumstances of the times, and for many drivers not used to the various types and ages of engines taken over by the War Department for military use.

Steam engines needed access to plentiful supplies of water and coal. It could take up to four hours to get steam up from cold. Rail gun routes had to take this into account as engines had to be kept in steam even when not moving. Stations in Britain had water stops about 35 miles (56km) apart. Where there was a connection to the mains, water cranes stood on station platforms. In some rural areas wind pumps filled station tanks, which held about 20,000 gallons (91,000 litres). The tender for the much-used 0-6-0 Dean Goods locomotive which hauled the rail guns held 3,000 gallons (14,000 litres) of water and 5 tons of coal. The coal bunkers in tenders had an inclined bottom so that the engine vibration brought the coal down within reach of the fireman. Mindful of the importance of this fuel the Government had told the railway companies to establish coal reserves in goods yards and sidings. It was the practice for long 'block trains' full of coal to be run from the collieries so that loaded wagons could be dropped off at stations. Many of these Government dumps were in Kent and Sussex. Firemen usually had to fill their tenders by shovel and it was easier to do this straight from a loaded coal wagon in a siding.

The Royal Engineer drivers of locomotives had to abide by the rules and procedures in the *Military Railway Rule Book*. These were similar to those established in 1842 by the Railway Clearing House, an organisation for deciding all matters relating to traffic passing over the lines of different rail companies. The *Military Railway Rule Book* had 102 rules and covered the duties of drivers, guards and blockmen (signalmen). Engine drivers from the railway companies conscripted into the army would have been familiar already with many of the procedures and safety measures, which were similar to those used in their civilian job. They also had to be mindful of the difficulties of edging large guns around tight curves and through tunnels or under trees, to conceal them from air attack. Engines had to be kept with steam up which made them visible to air attacks even when not moving; thus some were fitted with condensing apparatus and pannier tanks. These reduced the escape of steam which gave away the position of the train to aircraft. Eventually diesel engines were found to be better and replaced the Dean locomotives for hauling guns about. When the gun trains were moved to new locations the journey was usually made at night both for security purposes and because there was less traffic if travel across main lines was necessary.

The speed at which the railway gun and its wagons moved depended on the class of locomotive which pulled it, engine braking power, strength of bridges and the curves and gradients of the track on which it travelled. There was no scientific method of computing this accurately because any guidance had to err on the side of safety to avoid derailment. A rough guide suggested that a maximum speed could be assessed as ten times the diameter of the driving wheel. For a Dean engine this would be 40mph (64km); however, given the weight of rail-mounted artillery its travelling speed would have been much lower and was probably less than 18 miles (28km) an hour. The heavy guns manned by the Royal Marines were ordered to move at only a few miles per hour because of the effect of their weight on bridges. Moving a railway gun about on a fixed track so that it could engage with a target many miles away caused several problems. For some 12-inch and 9.2-inch calibre guns, which could be traversed at right angles to the track, it was necessary to secure them with spade arms, cables and outriggers. It was a lengthy process, which suggests that the gun train was best kept on a stationary site and moved about as little as possible. Larger calibre guns (13.5-inches and above) with only a limited traverse action had to be pointed directly at the target, and curved spurs with the firing positions marked in degrees were needed; a basic but practical aiming device given that there was little else available for these old guns. Whether they would have been of any use is a matter of opinion, but some gunners on the spot at the time had their doubts.

An ex-Great Western 0-6-0 Dean Goods locomotive, armoured and camouflaged against ground and air attack in the Second World War.

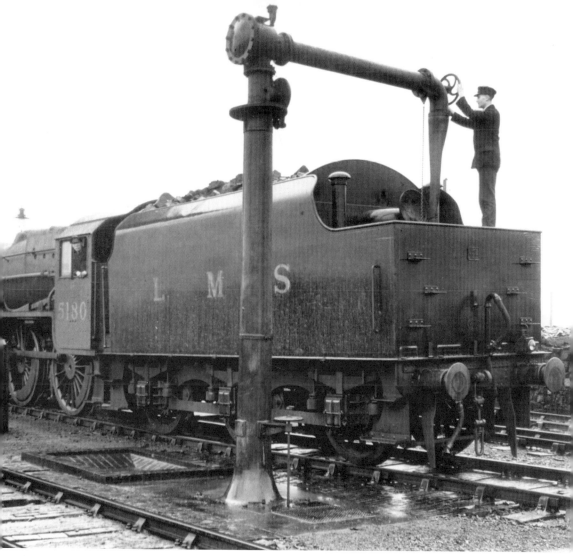

A water crane shoots water into a tender through a flexible hose.

An ex-Great Eastern F7, 2-4-2 tank locomotive painted in War Department camouflage. These locomotives were used on armoured trains that patrolled the East Coast of England. The trains were manned by Polish army crews.

Large capacity steam and diesel railway cranes were used when locomotives were derailed, or when gun barrels needed changing.

Cranes

For Supplying Locomotives with Water.

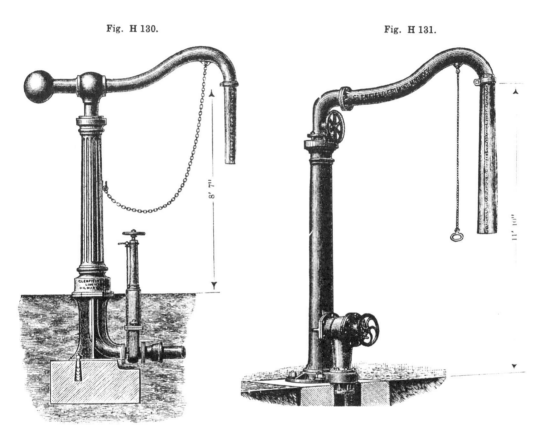

Fig. H 130.   Fig. H 131.

Types of water cranes, by Glenfield and Kennedy, iron founders of Kilmarnock, Scotland, found on station platforms for refilling tenders and water tanks of steam locomotives.

Royal engineers strengthened and laid railway tracks, curves and spurs for railway guns.

Two 9.2-inch railway guns anchored down for firing from spurs alongside the mainline. These guns were seen at Wittersham Road and Rolvenden stations and at Golden Wood and Bargrave Wood on the Ashford to Hastings line. Ex-Great Western Dean Goods 0-6-0 locomotives with condensing gear pulled the gun trains.

Southern Railway, Schools Class 4-4-0 901 Winchester is seen here in wartime black on a passenger train at Hildenborough cutting in 1946. Members of this class were sometimes used to move heavy guns along the Kent and Sussex coast in the Second World War. (John Scott-Morgan Collection)

Ex-Great Western Dean Goods 0-6-0 Tender Goods, WD 70094, on a troop train on the Shropshire & Montgomeryshire Light Railway, c.1945. These locomotives were used by the British Army in both world wars, to move and position railway guns in France, Belgium and on the South Coast. (John Scott-Morgan Collection)

Ex-Great Western Dean Goods 0-6-0 Tender Goods, WD 70093, at Kinnerley on the Shropshire & Montgomeryshire Light Railway, c.1947. The Dean Goods locomotives were originally used to haul railway guns on the south coast. (John Scott-Morgan Collection)

Chapter 7

Railway Gun Positions in Kent and Sussex

Kent

General Sir Andrew Thorne, known to his friends as Bulgy, had a distinguished career in the First World War, was rapidly promoted, and in June 1940 was the general in command of XII Corps spread out along the coast of Kent and Sussex. In his headquarters at Tunbridge Wells he was advised by his divisional artillery brigadiers to use the 13.5-inch Super Heavy railway batteries to support the static artillery on the South Foreland for counter battery fire across the Channel. The 18-inch, 12-inch and 9.2-inch railway guns were to destroy enemy forces approaching the beaches and to cover any retreat inland from the coast. With the few artillery pieces available this was the best use for them, although visiting commanders were well aware that being old First World War siege guns their performance was less than satisfactory for the purpose. Moreover the heaviest guns had a limited traverse of only a few degrees and were not suitable for firing at moving targets at sea. Railway spurs with curves had to be laid to overcome their limitations, but this could only be partially successful given the time it took to get them into action.

Army engineers put down new tracks, from Martin Mill station on the Kearsney Loop to Deal line, and across a golf course on the cliffs of the South Foreland. Powerful fixed 14- and 15-inch static guns emplaced here commanded the Dover Straits and French coast, and spurs enabled railway guns to fire on an enemy approaching the harbour and beaches.

It is fortunate that the Kent railway system, which radiated from the hub towns of Canterbury and Ashford, enabled railway guns to move about freely 20 miles (32km) back from the coast. Six railway lines radiating from Canterbury and five from Ashford allowed for alternative routes in the event of a withdrawal further inland being necessary. Limiting factors were the condition of some of the lines, the need for concealment from air attack and the availability of workshops for gun barrel changing and repairs. The ponderous nature of the heavier guns also meant that once in position it would take much time and effort to move them.

In 1940 only three Super Heavy Regiments with thirteen railway batteries had been formed after Dunkirk. The 1st Regiment was at Levington on the East Coast to cover the Harwich sector, although it was later transferred to join the 2nd and 3rd Super Heavy Regiments in Kent. General Lloyd's report to the War Cabinet had concluded that an invasion was most likely in the south of England. The railway batteries usually had two guns each, although the number deployed depended on how many were operational and where the Divisional Headquarters wanted them to be. The policy of XII Corps was to position most railway guns inland where they could fire on different parts of the long Kent coastline, which stretched from Whitstable to Dungeness. Beaches, cliff tops and the harbours of Ramsgate, Dover and Folkestone had to be covered so there was inevitably a certain amount of movement when batteries were exchanged for training, repair or strategic reasons. In the event of railway artillery having to retreat inland they were expected to destroy road and rail junctions between Ramsgate and Folkestone.

The railway lines from Canterbury

One of the most significant lines for railway gun movements was the 17-mile (27km) long Elham Valley line from Harbledown Junction south of Canterbury West station. It ran along the valley bottom and through the North Downs to join the main Southern Railway line at Cheriton outside Folkestone. Mainly single track, part was alongside the B2065 and over bridges on the River Nailbourne. In 1940 this line was closed to civilian traffic and reserved for military use. The 1st London Infantry, responsible for defending the Kent coast, used it to connect their many camps and units in the area. There was much movement of artillery in and out of the district and the 9.2-inch and 12-inch railway guns of the 2nd Super Heavy Regiment and Y Battery of the Canadian Royal artillery were seen on this line. Station buildings housed the battery HQ. Sheltered from the sea by high ground railway guns could hide unseen in tunnels at Bishopsbourne and Etchinghill. The 18-inch monster howitzer (*Boche Buster*) could be elevated to 40 degrees but had a limited traverse of only 2 degrees left and right so firing spurs were needed to point it directly at its target. The engineers laid a spur at Charlton Park near Kingston, aimed towards the sea between Ramsgate and Deal. This howitzer arrived in Kent in 1941 and was manned by the Royal Marines, but spent much of its time hiding in Bourne Park tunnel. Firing spurs were usually well camouflaged to hide them from aerial observation. This was done by stretching heavy wire fish netting in 35-foot squares over poles and garnishing them with hessian strips. These were issued in 100-yard rolls in four colours; dark green, light green, light earth and brown. There were rules to be followed in fixing the garnishing to the netting so that the eventual pattern complemented the surroundings. The goods yard at Elham station on this line was used to park 9.2-

inch and 12-inch howitzers of the Canadian artillery and the 2nd Super Heavy Regiment. Here, and at Lyminge, the coast between Hythe and Folkestone 8 miles away was within reach of the guns.

A colliery line from Canterbury West station went almost directly to Minster Junction. Along this line the Canadian Super Heavy Y Battery of 12-inch guns stood in sidings at Grove Ferry on the River Stour. Its job was to protect the Isle of Thanet and the North Foreland beaches 10 miles (16km) away.

The railway line from Canterbury East station went to Dover via Adisham, Shepherdswell and Kearsney Junction. It passed through mainly open undulating countryside with some tunnels and embankments. The straightness of the line close to Bekesbourne may be the reason the 18-inch (*Boche Buster*) spent time here as it pointed directly towards the Downs off Deal 16 miles (29km) away. There was continual military traffic on this line especially at Shepherdswell where Stonehall Colliery was used for parking engines, guns and changing gun barrels. Nearby Guston and Lydden tunnels were used to conceal ammunition trains and supplies for the South Foreland batteries. Most of the railway regiments including those manned by the Royal Marine siege regiments with their 13.5-inch guns and howitzers were on this line in the 1940s. Their orders were to protect Pegwell Bay and destroy the Dover harbour installations if they were captured.

At Shepherdswell junction on the Canterbury West line to Dover, the old East Kent Railway line, 14 miles (22km) long, curved away into a cutting and through the 477-yard (436m) long Golgotha tunnel to emerge on the outskirts of Eythorne. The tunnel was often used to shelter the 12-inch rail guns belonging to the 8th Battery. Most of the single-track line with passing loops ran through farmland serving several working coalmines, fruit and vegetable farms and brickworks. The stations were basic, with platforms, sidings and little else. At Eastry the line curved towards Ash, Staple and Wigham Town station, and ended in sidings, which may or may not have been built for the railway guns. The 0-6-0 Dean Goods locomotives used as their base the disused colliery sidings at Guilford on a branch line from Eythorne. Within a few miles of the coast the 9.2-inch and 12-inch guns, which trundled along the line had a range of up to 11 miles (20km), allowing them to cover a wide area of flat seashore between Herne Bay and Sandwich. The engineers laid down new sidings at Eythorne, Staple and Poulten Farm. Sidings were also needed for the wagons and coaches which accompanied the gun trains. Some reinforcement of the track was carried out where it was used for the rail guns to be anchored with clamps and guys when firing at right angles to the track. The 0-6-0 Dean Goods locomotives hauled the guns about and used the disused colliery sidings at Guilford, on a branch line at Eythorne, for their accommodation coaches. The 5th, 8th, 12th and 16th batteries of the 2nd Super Heavy Regiment travelled on this line for practice shots out to sea.

The railway lines from Ashford

From Hythe on the Kent coast, flat sand and shingle beaches stretch westward towards Dungeness, Rye and the Pett Levels where the cliffs begin again. The German XIII and VII corps planned to land their armies in this area.

South of Ashford station on the banks of the East Stour River was the Southern Region railway engineering works. The 3rd Super Heavy Battery with two 9.2-inch guns arrived at Ashford from the north in August 1940 and fortunately escaped an air raid on the works near the town. Pulled by a Dean 0-6-0 locomotive it moved down the Ashford to Folkestone line to firing positions on the coast at Hythe and Folkestone. On this line was a firing spur at Servington covering the flat coastline of Dungeness Bay 10 miles (16km) away across the Romney marshes. Between Servington and Sellindge the line passed through several cuttings which afforded some cover from air attacks. At Sandling junction a branch line went through cuttings to Hythe and a 9.2-inch gun (Cleeve) was here for a time. The main line from the junction continued through Cheriton to Folkestone and it was on this line that this railway gun got permission to fire at some German E-boats, but with no result. About 2 miles (3km) back from the coast at Newington on the Dover line there were firing positions at Bargrove Wood, and tunnels and cuttings from which guns could be hidden to put dropping fire onto the beaches.

A second line from Ashford station followed the edge of the Romney and Walland marshes only a few feet above sea level and about 8 miles (13km) from the coast. Sidings and cuttings were available at Kingsnorth, Golden Wood, Hollybush Farm and Ham Street, which, with camouflage net kits carried by the guns, could be used to conceal them. Railway guns of the 15th Battery of the 2nd Super Heavy Regiment and the Canadian X Battery travelled on this line with their 9.2-inch and 12-inch howitzers. These had a range of up to 12 miles (19km). Practice firing out to sea also took place on this line. A dummy gun to deceive the enemy was set up near Ruckinge level crossing. The beaches between Folkestone harbour and the east side of the Dungeness peninsula were also within range.

East Sussex

The first station north of Ashford on the Maidstone line was Hothfield where a reserve position for heavy rail-mounted guns had been established in sidings at a stone terminal. From this point the coastline between Folkestone and Dungeness was within range.

Another main Southern Railway line from Ashford to Tonbridge and Redhill passed through Headcorn where sidings connected it with the Kent and East Sussex Light Railway. This tortuous single line with tight curves wound its way through small towns and across the flood plain of the River Rother to

Robertsbridge. There were speed and weight restrictions on this line, only one cutting and a short tunnel on the outskirts of Tenterden. Two small corrugated iron stations, Rolvenden and Wittersham Road, had goods yards and sidings suitable for parking rail-mounted artillery and their accommodation coaches. The guns were here until 1944. From positions on this railway line 9.2-inch guns of the 4th Super Heavy Battery could fire across the marshes to the coast, reaching the Dungeness peninsula, Winchelsea Beach and Rye harbour. The shock wave when the guns fired out to sea is said to have broken windows in nearby houses.

Only two railway batteries were assigned for the protection of the rest of East Sussex and then not until June 1941 when 18th and 19th Super Heavy Batteries, each with two 12-inch howitzers arrived from the West Country. They were to stay for a year before being disbanded. Hereabouts the high cliffs of the South Downs protected much of the coast and railway guns were sited to bring down fire on the gaps in the hills made by the rivers Cuckmere and Ouse, west of Eastbourne. Several firing spurs were laid down a few miles back from the coast to keep the main line free.

At Glynde, on the Eastbourne to Lewes Southern Railway line, two spurs enabled howitzers to fire over the Downs to the Brighton beaches, and towards Newhaven harbour at the bottom of the Ouse valley. They also covered a joint naval and army underground plotting centre dug beneath South Heighton Hill, now sealed off but still there today. There was little cover and no tunnels on this line so camouflage had to be improvised in the few cuttings.

A single spur line was put down at Hellingly and two at Hailsham, both on the Southern Railway line from Eastbourne via Polegate to Edenbridge. These firing positions were to counter a possible advance of the 16th German army, which planned to land between Eastbourne and Folkestone. Cover from air attack on this line was limited to two cuttings although there was a lot of woodland.

West Sussex

The long flat and shallow open beaches west of Brighton were ideal for the landing of tanks and infantry of the 9th German army. The British and Canadian field artillery of the 38th and 47th divisions protecting this part of the coast was sited 2–3 miles inland on the South Downs and their lower slopes. Their task was to support infantry opposing the enemy where a beach landing might take place, and stop any advance inland. The closeness of West Sussex to Royal Navy ships from Portsmouth naval base meant that the coast hereabouts was continuously patrolled. There were also minefields and protective net barriers stretching for 22 miles (35km) out at sea. The 6-inch coast batteries, 7 miles (11km) apart, gave some additional security. Fire orders came from Fortress HQ at Newhaven and the naval officer there had the final say. There seems to have been no Super Heavy railway guns in West Sussex during the early stages of a possible invasion threat probably because the few available had already been allocated elsewhere, mainly to the Kent coast. In 1941 however the 14th Super Heavy Battery of 9.2-inch guns moved from Wareham, Dorset to Oaklands Park, Chichester. Its task was to neutralize the airfield on Thorney Island 7 miles away if it was captured by troop-carrying gliders. Later two 12-inch railway howitzers replaced this battery and were sited at Chichester station. Three firing spurs had to be built for them, two north of the main line and one on the south side. Just west of the town a single-track railway branched off from the main Brighton to Portsmouth line for Midhurst. Railway guns could travel up the Lavant Valley as far as Singleton station for firing exercises from the sidings. The distance from here to the sea off Bognor Regis was about 10 miles (16km). The three tunnels and cuttings on this line at West Dean, Singleton and Cocking provided excellent cover and were also used by the navy for storing wagonloads of mines and ammunition needed for their ships at Portsmouth. The stations on this little-used line were closed to passenger traffic in 1935 and to freight in 1953 so most of the traffic in the Second World War was military. There is no evidence that the railway guns in West Sussex ever fired other than in practice.

Ex-SER 0 class tender good locomotive, number 6, at one of the stations on the East Kent railway when it was used by railway guns in the 1940s for maintenance and gun barrel exchanges at Stonehall colliery nearby.

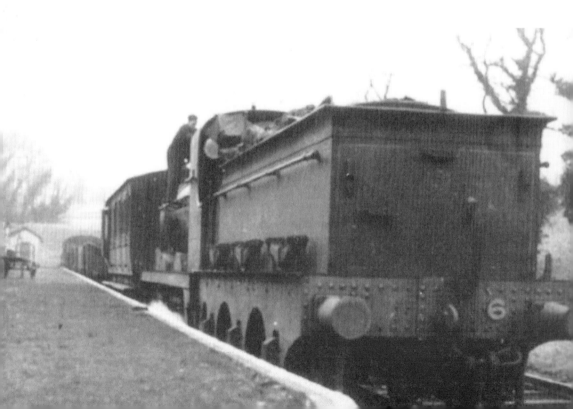

A gunner guides an approaching locomotive to couple up with an 18-inch railway mounted howitzer. (Author's Collection)

9.2-inch railway guns travelled over most lines in Kent. This one, anchored down with cables, was on the coast near Hythe.

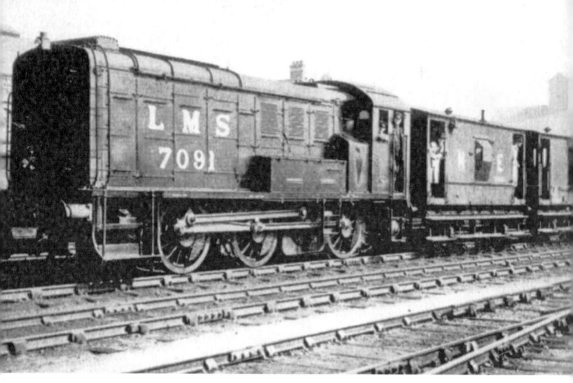

Diesel electric locomotives numbered 7090 and 7091 with a jackshaft transmission were built for the War Department in 1940. (Author's Collection)

The track layout at Polegate in 1940, which allowed rail guns to move between firing spurs at Hailsham and Glynde near Lewes.

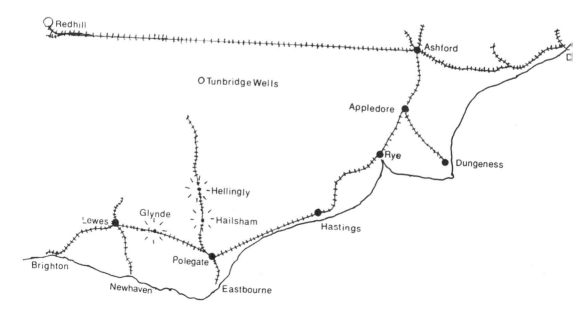

One of the tunnels on the former Midhurst line which was once used by railway guns and ammunition trains for the Royal Navy at Portsmouth.

Firing spurs outside Chichester station (X) and sidings (Y) for railway guns, 8 miles from their target areas on the coast.

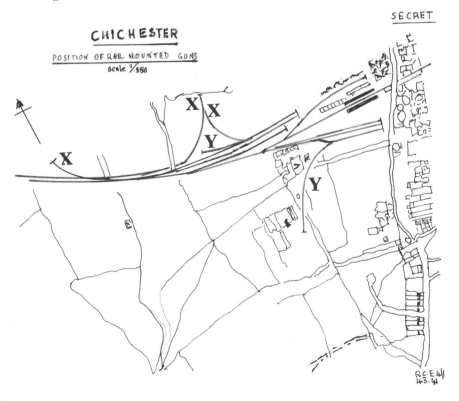

Adjusting the shell hoist of an 18-inch railway howitzer.

Prime Minister Winston Churchill inspects a 13.5-inch railway mounted howitzer on the Kent coast. In the foreground are the spade arms and chains which anchor the gun when it fires.

One of the gun observation posts at Dover, staffed by both navy and army personnel to coordinate the fire of batteries along the coast and ensure no friendly ships were fired upon.

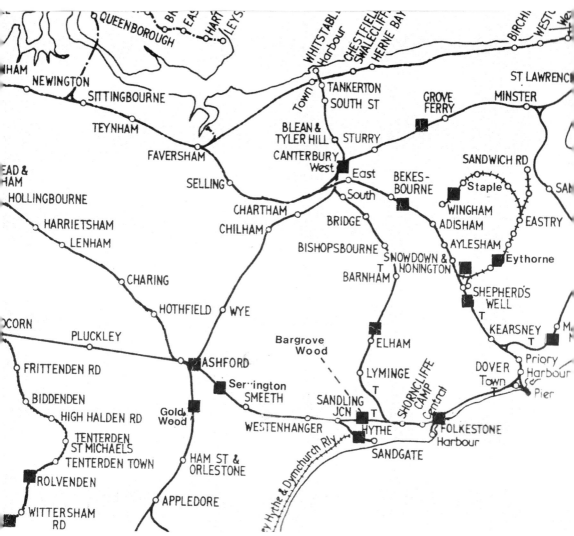

The railway network in Kent as it existed in the Second World War. A black square marks the various positions taken up by railway mounted guns to cover beaches and road junctions. Tunnels for hiding the guns are shown with a 'T'.

Chapter 8

Command of the Dover Straits

On windswept chalk downland close to the South Foreland cliffs stands the insignificant Martin Mill station on the Southern Railway line from the Kearsney–Dover loop line to Ramsgate. In 1940 its goods yard became of great importance to the security of England and it was used extensively for railway guns and batteries guarding the Dover Straits.

An old military railway line had been laid from the goods yard in 1897 to take ballast down the cliff for the building of Dover Admiralty harbour. It fell into disuse and was removed in the late 1930s. After the evacuation of the army from Dunkirk and fears about German domination of the Straits army engineers hastily relaid and extended this line to bring very heavy guns and ammunition to new emplacements being dug out of the chalk behind the South Foreland cliffs. One extension line branched off at RDF (Radio Direction Finding station) Junction to service the static 14-inch gun sites of *Winnie* and *Pooh*. This line ended beyond Hog's Bush. Also off this line were spurs for more railway guns to fire seawards. A second extension about 1,400 yards (1km) nearer the sea continued past new 15-inch gun positions at Wanstead Farm and over a level crossing on the road leading to St Margaret's Bay. It ended in farmland to accommodate the 13.5-inch hyper-velocity railway gun *Bruce*.

The construction work, steel girders to support the *Winnie* and *Pooh* gun mountings and cradles, weighing nearly 100 tons, caused problems as the work was being done while there were constant air raids on nearby Dover. The extensive rail network in this area was essential for serving the fixed gun positions, changing gun barrels and bringing up heavy shells.

The small Martin Mill goods yard was crammed with Dean Goods and diesel shunting engines, brake vans and Warflat wagons carrying rails. Locomotives were used to move the heavy gun mountings into their fixed position in the gun pits and to trundle the railway guns to the firing spurs. There were eventually over thirty guns on the South Foreland in fixed emplacements, their purpose being twofold: to counter-bombard German heavy artillery batteries and railway guns on the French coast, and to stop enemy ships and convoys attempting to run through the 21-mile (33km) Dover Straits. Smaller 6-inch guns on the cliffs were sited to fire on invasion ships and landing craft approaching the shore.

There was a lot of activity at the Martin Mill goods yard, undertaken against a background of constant air raids and so much shelling from German heavy guns, that in Dover the town's air raid sirens sounded a second warning after the first to signal if there were incoming shells from artillery. The engines which hauled the guns had to be serviced in the open. Locomotives shifted the 13.5-inch railway guns mounted on box carriages (*Gladiator*, *Piecemaker* and *Scene Shifter*) in and out of the Guston tunnel and onto the firing spurs as necessary. Shells and cordite were brought to the magazines in armoured railway wagons. Some F1 Class 4-4-0 engines (1457 and 1459) were kept in the yard with steam up. Their trucks were loaded with concrete to block Guston tunnel if an invasion began. Steam cranes from Guildford and Kings Cross were needed from time to time to change the gun barrels of the fixed heavies, *Winnie* and *Pooh*.

The extension line from Martin Mill that was laid past the 15-inch static gun positions, through the clifftop village of St Margaret's at Cliffe and out past Hog's Bush, was occupied by the one-off monster rail gun *Bruce*. This was an experimental hyper-velocity gun with a 16-inch barrel with a liner reducing its calibre to 8-inches. It was mounted on a box carriage and when fired its shells could reach a range of 70 miles (112km) although a new gun barrel was needed after every twenty-eight rounds. For test firing it was always aimed east towards the Shoeburyness ranges bordering the North Sea but it never fired at the enemy. Dummy gun positions and railway tracks were built to deceive the enemy about the exact positions of the *Winnie* and *Pooh* batteries.

Prime Minister Winston Churchill took a keen personal interest in ensuring that the defences at Dover were strong. His constant pressure on General Ismay to see that this was done no doubt caused grumbles amongst the military hierarchy, but his vision was clear. Britain and not Germany must dominate and control the Dover Straits and to do this the area must be stuffed with guns whatever their efficiency. This was achieved. His second objective, to destroy the forty-odd batteries on the French shore at Cap Gris-Nez before they got established was not achieved and was probably impossible anyway because of the more powerful nature of the German artillery and the resources devoted to making their emplacements impregnable. Eventually both sides settled down to occasional bursts of shelling – Dover town suffered most with 1,000 properties destroyed and more damaged by shelling and air raids. Over 2,000 shells are reported to have fallen on the town causing over 200 civilian deaths and 800 injured.

Most of the artillery and their gunners, including the railway guns, escaped. There were some near misses to the fixed guns and *Pooh*'s ready-use magazine was hit. If railway lines were blown up they were quickly relaid. None of the railway guns seem to have been badly damaged and it is likely they spent most of the time hidden in Guston tunnel. To get them out and into action was a lengthy business.

The Wanstone 15-inch counter-bombardment battery, able to fire onto the French coast. The railway line served other batteries, brought up shells and replaced gun barrels.

The 14-inch counter -bombardment battery, Winnie, concealed in a deep gun pit. Its shell could reach the German batteries on the French coast.

The 9.2-inch railway gun, introduced by Elswick Co in the First World War, continued in service until 1945. It had a range of 12 miles and was often in sidings along the Kent and Sussex coast.

Views of Martin Mill station on the South Foreland. The shunting yard and specially laid military railway to the gun positions was south of the station.

COMPARISON DETAILS FOR SOME RAILWAY MOUNTED GUNS ON THE WESTERN FRONT IN WW1

Country	Equipment	Gun or Howitzer	Date in Service	Maximum Elevation Degrees	Maximum Traverse Degrees	Shell weight (Kg)	Maximum Range (metres)
America	14-inch/50 calibre	Gun	1918	43	2.5 left & right	640kg	38,000 metres/23 miles
Britain	9.2-inch Mark 10	Gun	1916	30	360	172kg	19,200 metres/12 miles
Britain	12-inch Mark 1	Howitzer	1916	65	40	340kg	10,180 metres/6 miles
Britain	12-inch Mark 3	Howitzer	1916	65	40	340kg	13,700 metres/9 miles
Britain	12-inch Mark 9	Gun	1915	30	2	385kg	29,900 metres/19 miles
France	Canon 164mm	Gun	1893	36	depends on mounting	51kg	18,000 metres/11 miles
France	Canon 240mm	Gun	1915	35	360	162kg	22,700 metres/14 miles
France	Mortar 293mm	Howitzer	1915	N/A	N/A	N/A	N/A
France	Canon 305mm	Gun	1893–1896	40	depends on mounting	348kg	31,000 metres/19 miles
France	Obusier 400mm	Howitzer	1915–1916	65	12	641kg	16,000 metres/10 miles
France	Obusier 520mm	Howitzer	1916	60	none	1,500kg +	17,000 metres/11 miles
Germany	15cm SK ('Nathan')	Gun	1916	45	50/180	44kg	22,675 metres/14 miles
Germany	17cm SK L/40 ('Samual')	Gun	1917	45	26	64kg	24,000 metres/14 miles
Germany	21cm SK ('Peter Adalbert')	Gun	1916–1918	45	2	Case	26,000 metres/16 miles
Germany	24cm SK/L ('Theodor Otto')	Gun	1918	45	4	Case	18,700 metres/12 miles
Germany	24cm SK L/40 ('Theodor Karl') Howitzer	Howitzer	1916	45	180	151kg	26,600 metres/16 miles
Germany	28cm SK/L 40 ('Bruno')	Howitzer	1917	45	180	Case	27,500 metres/17 miles
Germany	28cm SK/L40 ('Kurfust')	Gun	1918	45	180	240kg	25,900 metres/16 miles
Germany	38cm SK/L 45 ('Max')	Gun	1918	18.5	2	750kg	47,500 metres/29 miles

Mounting platforms for railway guns. (Top) Warflat (Middle) Warwell (Bottom) Cradle, box.

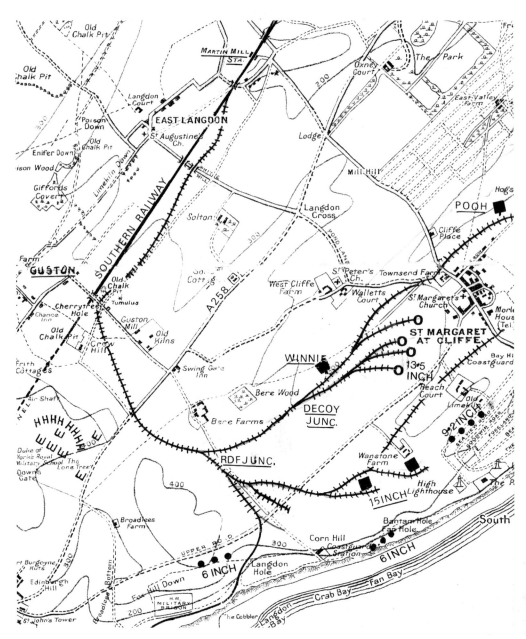

The military railway line from Martin Mill station across the South Foreland to the fixed gun positions and firing spurs for railway guns.

A 24cm 'Theodor Bruno' railroad gun, showing details of the Vögele turntable and the circular traversing track.

The largest and nearly the last of the Second World War railroad guns was the 80cm (E) 'Dora', which was called 'Schwerer Gustav' from 22 June 1922. Here, 'Dora' moves in its prepared firing position, which has been enclosed by barbed wire fences, secured and camouflaged for several kilometres in each direction, to help conceal the large weapon from enemy observation, air attacks and Russian naval vessels.

With captured and surrendered guns, the operational stocks of German railway guns were expanded after 1940. Here are two 30.5cm railroad guns, M93/06, in a railway station in the West in 1940.

Taken from the French, this 320mm H74 (f) Railway Howitzer from the rear left side, showing the relatively modern carriage design and the two 5-axle end bogie trucks.

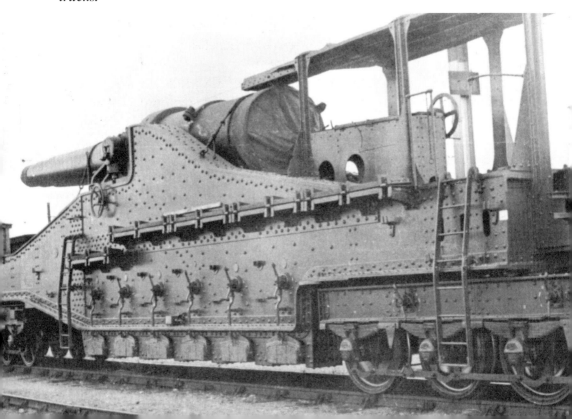

Chapter 9

German Railway Guns and Cross-Channel Bombardment Batteries

Calais to Boulogne

Heavy German artillery of all calibres began to be installed on the French coast overlooking the Straits of Dover from the summer of 1940. This was because Hitler, in Directive No 16 (July) had ordered that heavy guns should dominate and protect the coast in preparation for a surprise invasion of England. This was to take place on a broad front between Ramsgate in Kent and the Isle of Wight. 'The largest possible number of guns must be installed as soon as possible to safeguard the crossing and to cover both flanks against enemy intervention.' As preparations began to implement his orders railway mounted guns capable of shelling Kent moved to the coast in August. Several stayed permanently, but in 1941 others were withdrawn for the Russian Front. With German thoroughness dome- or cathedral-shaped bunkers were built or excavated close to the firing spurs to hide them and their locomotives from air attack. Each bunker was capable of holding two railway guns and one locomotive.

The same Directive required the Todt building organisation to construct massive concrete emplacements for very large guns. Under this programme five emplacements, with magazines and crew quarters for guns capable of bombarding the Kent coast, were built close to the sea between Boulogne and Calais. As some were to be armed with ex-naval battleship guns not all became operational immediately, even after the emplacements were ready:

Batterie Oldenburgh, 2 x 240mm (9.5-inch) guns with a range of 27km (16 miles) built to the east of Calais.

Batterie Lindemann, 3 x 406mm (15-inch) guns with a range of 56km (34 miles) near Sangatte.

Batterie Kurfrst, 4 x 280mm (11-inch) guns with a range of 30km (18 miles) to the east of Cap Gris-Nez.

Batterie Todt, 4 x 380mm (15-inch) guns with a range of 48km (29 miles) south of Cap Gris-Nez.

Batterie Friedrich August, 3 x 305mm (12-inch) guns with a range of 51km (31 miles) near Wimereux.

These very heavy casemated gun positions were able to sink shipping in the Dover Straits, and three could bombard the British gun sites on the South Foreland. In design, size, strength and thickness of concrete the German defence structures built by the Todt organisation were better protected than those on the Dover cliffs which might be described as shoddy works by comparison. However, as Britain kept its control over the Straits it is evident that its gun batteries were up to the job at lesser cost in money and manpower resources.

The German army was well provided with different types of Super Heavy railway guns which were essential for fighting land and border battles and despite their weight could travel faster than by road on the excellent European railway networks.

German railway artillery was classified as K (kone: gun) with a number. The German armament manufacturer Krupp built about twenty-five K5 and two K12 (E) railway guns in the Second World War. Several of these were sent to the Pas de Calais area while the more permanent casemated gun emplacements were being built. Hitler never gave the order to invade and after 1944 the railway guns were needed instead to oppose a British invasion which was expected to cross over the Dover Straits.

The railway batteries remaining the longest in the Pas de Calais area were armed with K5 and K12 (E) guns with the following characteristics:

K5 was a railway gun with a calibre of 283mm (11 inch). It was 30m (98 feet) in length, weighed 215 tons and was mounted on a fixed box girder mounting which rested on two bogies with twenty-four wheels. When elevated it could fire a shell weighing 255kg (563lbs) over 64km (40 miles).

K 12 (E) was a much longer-range gun with a calibre of 211mm (11-inch). It was 33m (109 feet) in length, weighed 298 tons and was able to fire a standard high explosive shell over 115km (71 miles). There are reports of shell fragments being picked up near Chatham in Kent, Dover, and Eastbourne in Sussex, all places over 80km (50 miles) from the French coast. This gun was also mounted on a box girder carriage carried by four sets of bogies with thirty-six wheels. It had a cleverly designed pneumatic recoil mechanism which allowed it to elevate to 55 degrees. One disadvantage was the length of its barrel which had to be braced to prevent it bending.

As with most railway guns the German ones also had a limited traverse. They had to be manoeuvred along curved spurs to point them in line with the target, which made them useless for firing at moving targes such as ships. To overcome this restriction most German rail guns carried a portable turntable (*Vogel*

Drehscheibe) onto which the railway gun could be moved, allowing it to traverse 360 degrees. They also used a prefabricated cross-T-shaped track arrangement laid so that the bogies were at right angles for firing when clamped down. But both these methods were time consuming to set up and the latter even needed a special crane wagon to accompany the train. The cumbersome operations involved found little favour with the gunners.

The make-up of a German railway train was not much different from the British, although perhaps better designed and equipped, and certainly more modern. For each battery of two guns there were usually two steam locomotives, although smokeless diesels were preferred as they did not attract the attention of aircraft. The railway guns deployed to fire across the Dover Straits supported the guns in the fixed emplacements.

German railway guns in 1940 were well engineered, more recent and generally superior in fire power to those of the British. As has already been mentioned attention had also been given to overcoming problems of traversing the gun. Turntables giving a 360-degree traverse were standard equipment for each gun and an efficient suspension mechanism on the carriage allowed it to move easily on temporary and poorly constructed railway tracks.

It is ironic that the guns on this part of the French coast (intended to safeguard the German Sealion invasion fleet from the Royal Navy) saw their role reversed from an offensive to a defensive one after 1941 when Hitler postponed the invasion indefinitely.

Following the breakout of the Allied armies from Normandy in September 1944 the coast batteries were deemed to be too strong to be attacked from the sea. General Montgomery asked the First Canadian Army to attack the German gun positions on the Cap Gris-Nez coastline. He wanted supplies for his 21st army group to come through the strongly guarded ports of Calais and Boulogne and also to put a stop to the shelling of Dover. Attacked from the land side and isolated, capture was inevitable and many second-class troops, who in this late stage of the war manned the batteries, gave up without much of a fight. The fate of the railway guns is unknown but it is likely that they were withdrawn much earlier before a land attack on the coastal defences began.

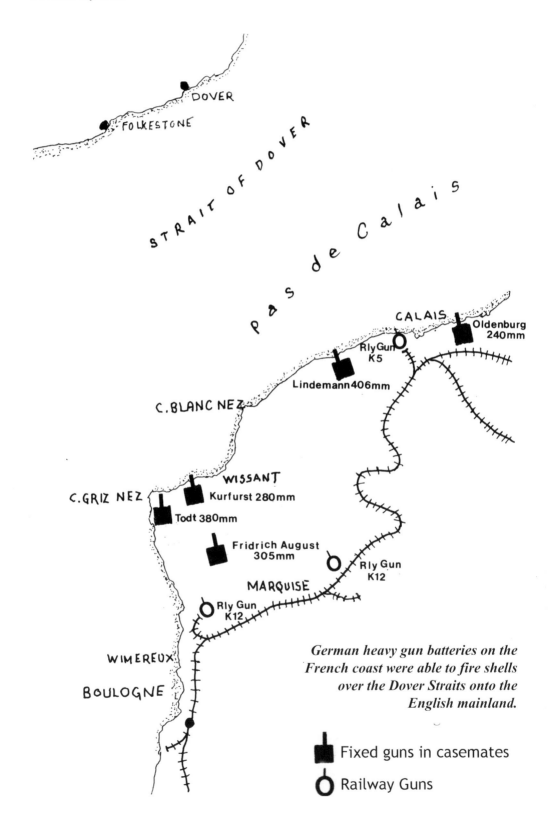

DOVER

FOLKESTONE

STRAIT OF DOVER

Pas de Calais

CALAIS

Oldenburg
240mm

Rly Gun
K5

Lindemann 406mm

C. BLANC NEZ

WISSANT

Kurfurst 280mm

C. GRIZ NEZ

Todt 380mm

Fridrich August
305mm

Rly Gun
K12

MARQUISE

Rly Gun
K12

WIMEREUX

BOULOGNE

German heavy gun batteries on the French coast were able to fire shells over the Dover Straits onto the English mainland.

■ Fixed guns in casemates

O Railway Guns

German dome bunkers were built near the coast where there was no other cover. Here a railway gun can be seen in the entrance.

The clean design of the (1940) K 5 (E) 283mm railway gun with a range of 23 miles.

Battery Todt near Cap Griz-Nez on the French Channel Coast, with a 380mm heavy naval gun adapted by Krupp for coast defence installed. Max range was 40 miles (64km).

This dome bunker, which could house two railway guns and a locomotive, was built on a spur line at Cap Griz-Nez.

A K5 283mm railway gun with its barrel lowered and shell hoist visible at the rear. It had a range of 40 miles (64km).

A K5 283mm railway gun with its 72-foot (22-metre) gun barrel lowered for travel through a goods yard.

The rear of Battery Todt, showing the entry portal.

A 380mm railway gun mounted on a Vögele Drehscheibe turntable, allowing it to be turned around to fire through 360 degrees.

A German K12 210mm railway gun with its guns barrel jacked up into the firing position. Weighing 318 tons, it had a range of 71 miles (113km).

A German WWI 17cm ex naval gun, **Samual** *mounted on a geared rail on a railway carriage allowing it to traverse 26 degrees.*

Chapter 10

The Final Salvos
of Guns on the Coast

Following the conquest of France the entire British coastline became a front line facing the enemy. The beaches of Kent and Sussex were the most likely to be invaded because of the shortest sea crossing from the French coast. A decision was taken to site gun batteries in brick and concrete emplacements about every 7–10 miles (11–16km) along the coast where there were no high cliffs. Most batteries comprised two 6-inch guns although a severe shortage of artillery led to older 4-inch and 5.5-inch guns being installed. The total number of *fixed* coast batteries has never been counted successfully but there were about sixty in Kent and twenty-two in Sussex. Batteries of field artillery sited well back from the sea backed these up. As no invasion was ever attempted most guns, with the exception of those at Dover, never opened fire at an enemy other than at E-boats and other craft that looked suspicious and did not signal the password of the day.

With British naval ships patrolling the Channel the Admiralty were insistent that their freedom of movement should not be limited. They were wary of trigger-happy gunners on shore firing at their ships because of mistaken identity. Orders to fire were tightly controlled from joint army and naval plotting rooms at Portsmouth, Newhaven and Dover. The decision to fire coast guns, including railway guns, always rested with the senior naval officer in charge at these places.

At Dover, with fixed heavier guns on the South Foreland, enemy ships attempting to run through the Channel or sailing close to the French coast were often fired upon; 540 Coast Regiment with its 6-inch, 9.2-inch and 15-inch gun batteries are credited with sinking twenty-six enemy ships.

Against this record must be measured the usefulness of the railway guns. The heaviest, *Bruce*, with a range of 70 miles (114km) was never ordered to fire on the French coast. Possibly it was not thought worthwhile risking further retaliation on Dover town as aircraft bombing raids could do the job better. *Boche Buster*, sited inland to bombard the Kent landing beaches, was also never needed. The three 13.5-inch railway heavies from the First World War, *Scene Shifter*, *Gladiator* and *Piecemaker* sent from Catterick by Colonel Cleeve, and also possibly capable of bombarding the French shore spent much of the time sheltering in the Guston and Lydden tunnels. On one occasion in 1941, two of these guns were hauled into position on firing spurs and elevated to fire over 22 miles (35km) into Calais. It seems one gun jumped back 6 feet (1.8 metres), which meant repositioning took some time. After firing four rounds it then took two hours to get the guns back into the safety of Guston tunnel. Of the 12-inch and 9.2-inch railway guns only one seems to have engaged the enemy. This was a 9.2-inch railway gun (*Gee*) in Folkestone West station sidings, which was given permission to fire at German E-boats, spotted 14 miles (22km) off shore. The shell overshot and the recoil caused the gun to come off the rails.

Air power, and the mobility and firepower of modern guns had rendered railway artillery out of date and not fit for purpose. Always expensive items of military hardware, in the 1940s they were called back into service in desperation for the purpose of warning the enemy to keep away if he tried to invade. Fortunately they were never needed.

Despite some early thoughts on the matter no British railway guns followed the army to France on D-Day. Their heyday was in the First World War and their use afterwards minimal. All British coastal artillery was abolished in 1956.

British Railway Mounted Artillery

A simplified table of railway artillery details intended to highlight significant differences in weight, range, and type of truck and number of bogie sets for each gun is shown below. There were several methods of mounting the gun or howitzer on well, flat, and box trucks. These included pivots, turntables, slides, cradles and trunions. All were designed to absorb recoil and facilitate elevation and traverse action.

	Weight (tons)	Range (miles)	Truck Type (no of bogie sets)
9.2-inch gun Mk 3	60	-	Well 2 x 4-wheel bogies.
9.2-inch gun Mk 10	90	12	Flat 2 x 4-wheel bogies.
9.2-inch gun Mk 13	86	12	Flat 2 x 4-wheel bogies.
12-inch gun Mk 9	171	19	Box 3 x 4-wheel bogies.
13.5-inch gun Mk 5*	240	22	Box 2 x 4- 1 x 4- and 1 x 3-wheel bogies.
14-inch gun Mk 3	248	20	Box 1 x 6- and 3 x 8-wheel bogies.
12-inch how. Mk 1	58	6	Well 2 x 4-wheel bogies.
12-inch how. Mk 3	60	9	Well 2 x 4-wheel bogies.
18-inch how. Mk 1**	250	13	Box 1 x 6- and 3 x 8-wheel bogies.

Scene Shifter, Gladiator, Piecemaker.
** *Boche Buster*

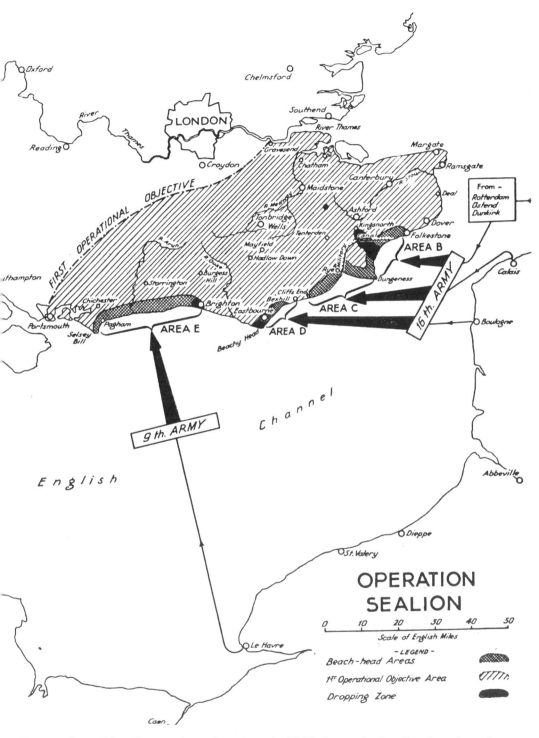

One version of the German invasion plans in 1940 shows the landing beaches of an advance towards the eventual capture of London.

Railway gun and crew on a curved firing spur near Dover in the 1940s. (Author's Collection)

Bibliography

Books:

Arnander, C., *Lord Crawford's War Diaries*, 2013

Arnold, B.E., *Conflict across the Strait*, 1982

Balfour, G., *The Armoured Train*, 1981

Cherry, N., *Battle of Loos*, 1915

Churchill, W., *WW2. Vol II Their Finest Hour*, 1949

Collyer, D.G., *Shellfire Memories*, 1993

Darwin, B., *War on the Line*, 1946

Delaforce, P., *Smashing the Atlantic War*, 2001

Doherty, R., *Ubique. Artillery in WW II*, 2008

Earnshaw, A., *British Railways at War 1914–1918*, 1990

Earnshaw, A., *British Railways at War 1939–1945*, 1995

Farndale, M., Gen. Sir., *Years of Defeat 1939–41*, 1996

Foynes, J.P., *Battle of the East Coast 1939–45*, 1994

Girouard, E., Sir, *Railways for Coast Defence*, 1891

Goodwin, J.E., *Defending Sussex Beaches 1940–42*, 2010

Hattendorf, J.B. & others, *British Naval Documents years 1204–1960* (Navy Records Society, 1993)

Headlam, J., Gen. Sir, *History of the Royal Artillery, 1860–1914*, 1937

Headlam, J., Gen. Sir, *History of the Royal Artillery*, Vol 3, 1940

Hogg, I.V., *Barrage*, 1970

Hogg, I.V., *Coast Defences of England and Wales*, 1974

Hogg, I.V., *German Artillery of WW II*, 1975

Hogg, I.V., *Guns of WW II*, 1976

Hogg, I.V., *Artillery of WW II*, 1978

Hogg, I.V. & Batchelor, J., *Railway Guns*, 1973

Hogg, I.V. & Thurston, L.F., *British Artillery 1914–1918*, 1972

Humphreys, R., *Hellfire Corner*, 1994

Hutton, J. (ed.), *A Doctor on the Western Front: The Diary of Dr Henry Owens 1914–18*, 2013

Hythe, Viscount, *The Naval Annual*, 1913

Ian, Allen, *British Railways Atlas 1947*, 2011

Jackson, A.A., *The Railway Dictionary A–Z*, 1996

James, N.D.G., *Gunners at Larkhill*, 1983

Jobson, P., *Artillery Terms and Abbreviations*, 2008

Kaufmann, J.E., *Fortress Europe*, 1999

Kaufmann, J.E., *Fortress Third Reich*, 2003

Khalla-Bishop, P.M., *Locomotives at War*, 1980

Litchfield, N.E. & Westlake, R., *Artillery Volunteers, 1859–1908*, 1982

Lloyd, E. & Hadcock, A., *Artillery Progress and Present*, 1893

Ludlam, A.J., *Catterick Camp Military Railway*, 1993

Lyne, R.M., *Military Railways in Kent*, 1983

Marshall Dendy, C.F., *History of Southern Railway*, 1963

Miller H.W., Lt. Col., *Railway Artillery: A Report on the Characteristics, Scope of Utility etc, Vol I, 1921*

Nicholson, C., Gen. Sir, *History of Royal Artillery 1919–39*, 1978

Royal Engineers Institution. *History of Royal Engineer Corps*, Vols 5, 7, 8, 1952

Ronald, D.W. & Carter, R.J., *Longmoor Military Railway*, 1974

Saunders, A., *Hitler's Atlantic Wall*, 2001

Showell, J.P.M., *Fuehrer Conferences on Naval Affairs 1939–1945*, 1990

Strong, P. & Saunders, M., *Artillery in the Great War*, 2011

Tourret, R., *War Department Locomotives*, 1976

Ventham, P. & Fletcher, D., *Moving the Guns: The Mechanisation of the Royal Artillery 1854–1939*, 1990

White, H.P., *Forgotten Railways* Vol 6, 1976

Wildish, G.N., *Engines of War*, 1946

Wrottesley, G., *Life & Letters of Sir John Burgoyne*, 1873

War Department Manuals:

26/103 *Railways*, 1929

40/WO/6049 *Artillery Training Vol. 3 War*, 1928

40/2292 *Garrison Artillery Training Vol. 2 Siege*, 1911

40/1312 *Field Artillery Training* (Prov), 1912

26/1886 *Coast Artillery Training* Vol 1, 1933

26/1082 *Coast Artillery Training* Vol II, 1934

26/1220 *Artillery Training Vol II Gunnery*, 1934

26/506 *Camouflage. Principles, Equipment & Materials*, 1941

Other sources of information:

Balfour, G., Correspondence on armoured trains in 1986

British Rail Press Office, 'Facts about BR in Wartime', 1943

British Rail Press Office, 'More about BR in Peace & War', 1945

British Rail Press Office, 'BR in Peace & War' 1947

Cleeve, S.M., *The Gunner* magazine, No 9, 1970

Cobb, P. (ed.), Wood, D., *Gazetteer of Forts & Batteries*, 2012

Fortnightly Review magazine, July–December 1895

Gittus, W.E.G., Correspondence on Railway Guns in 1983

Graphic newspaper 26 May 1894 (picture of Sussex gun train)

Hemans, A., Research on the early Sussex Railway Gun MSS with diagrams

Reed, J., 'Cross Channel Guns. After the Battle', No 29, 1980

The Times newspaper, 21 May 1896, 'Sussex Artillery Train'

Volunteer Service magazine, Numbers 25, 30, 57, 1894–97 (Sussex gun train picture)

The National Archive documents:

WO 196/33 'Report on Munitions', June 1940

WO 199/909 'Report to War Cabinet on invasion danger', 1940

(Scotland) C.19/53 28r–34r (Anderson – first railway gun)

Index